Dawdling
in the
Dale

Dedicated to my family

Wife Beryl
Son David
Daughter Charlotte

Published in 2015
by A T D Evans
Clun, Shropshire

A CIP record for this book is available from
the British Library
ISBN 978-0-9560569-1-7

Printed in England by Craven Design and Print Ltd

Dawdling
in the
Dale

A Photographic Study of the Social
and Local History in the
Rural Corvedale Valley

by

A T D EVANS

About the Author

Albert Thomas David Evans (alias **A**ttention **T**o **D**etail Evans) was born at Hawkestone House, 14 Market Street, Craven Arms, Shropshire on October 26th 1939, the second son of David and Nora (nee Thomas) Evans. David comes from a family which, in various capacities, has been involved in commerce for generations. His father and grandfather were smallholders at Whettleton Hill, Stokesay and both his great grandfather and great great grandfather were coal merchants (Samuel Chester & Son) with depots at railway stations in the area. The business later became C W Summerfield, Coal Merchant and Builders' Merchant in Station Drive, Craven Arms.

At fifteen, David left school, having been educated at Stokesay Primary School, Church Stretton Secondary School and Shrewbury Technical College. His father died in 1959 at the age of 52, leaving David to run the smallholding. A career shift in 1961 saw him opening a retail confectionery/greengrocery shop at the family home in Market Street, Craven Arms. Moving to 5,000 sq ft premises at Lower Market Street in 1971, David switched to retailing hardware, gardening and DIY products under the business name of Davy's Outpost. In 1981, the firm became a wholesale enterprise, changed its name to Border Distribution, and moved to a new base at Long Lane Industrial Estate, Craven Arms. Retirement came in 1999.

Unaccustomed idleness was soon overcome by a blossoming interest in local history and collecting Edwardian postcards of his home county and Mid Wales. This hobby has taken David all over the country – to second hand bookshops and car-boot sales, to junk shops, far flung auctions, and of course to postcard fairs. That led to giving illustrated talks and writing books. The first one being a pictorial history of the Welsh Marches, named 'Border Wanderings'.

David and his wife Beryl, who were married in 1966, first lived in the Corvedale near to Craven Arms, moving to Hopesay where they brought up their two children, David and Charlotte. After spending a happy 27 years in Hopesay, they moved to a new home in 2006, overlooking the castle ruins at Clun.

A.T.D. Evans (David)

Message from the Author

Working for the last six years on my book, 'Dawdling in the Dale', has been a wonderful experience for me, viewing some of the most glorious countryside in England, meeting with the local South Shropshire characters and listening to their stories. To set the scene I will describe the area geographically. The Corvedale consists of a wide flat valley flanked by Wenlock Edge to the north west and the Clee Hills to the south. It is in fact the most southernmost dale in England. Wenlock Edge, one of the most famous geological sites in the world, is a limestone escarpment created by crushed sea creatures and shellfish that once lived on a coral reef 425 million years ago (fossilised coral can still be found there to-day). It is some 18 miles long, running from Ironbridge to Craven Arms, and is now an attractive, tree covered ridge with old lime kilns and quarries, showing how industrial the area was in years gone by. Callow Hill is the highest peak of the Edge at 1085ft where Flounders Folly can still be found standing proudly to-day.

The hills to the south of the Corvedale are the Clee Hills. They consist of the Brown Clee and Titterstone Clee, which together, stretch fifteen miles running from north to south. Both are areas of outstanding natural beauty. Brown Clee is the highest peak of Shropshire at 1772ft above sea level and is situated five miles north of the Titterstone Clee. Abdon Burf is at Brown Clee's peak where mining has been carried out for many years. Dhustone (Dolerite), an extremely hard rock, was extracted up until 1936 when Adbon Clee quarries closed. Hill forts are dotted all over the hill and air traffic control radar masts are akin to candles on a giant cake, showing up for miles around. It is said that it is the highest land in an easterly direction until the Russian Ural mountains which perhaps is why the local Inn is named the Kremlin and why the masts pick up signals with little interference. Lord Boyne's Burwarton Estate covers much of the eastern slopes and private landowners, together with common land, covers the western side. The Corvedale valley, the broadest valley in the Shropshire Hills, is a fairly flat, fertile expanse that has been used mainly for sheep, cattle and arable farming. In the past, the alder trees along the river's edge, provided another profitable crop, clogs. Alders would be coppiced to provide clog soles that would be sold by the cloggers to the shoe finishers who attached a leather top, making a very suitable shoe, especially for workers in the steel industry.

There are many more characters and stories of the Corvedale but I have tried to present a Corvedale potted history, helped by my granddaughter Esme Evans who has been my Junior Administrative Assistant.

Now you have a picture of the area I will begin the trip down the river Corve.

David

List of Towns, Villages and Hamlets

Foreword

This book, **'Dawdling in the Dale'** is the second title the author has compiled, the first being **'Border Wanderings'**. That was a pictorial history of the Welsh Border Marches to the western side of the A49 trunk road. As in the first title, the idea was to use picture postcards that had been taken by a local photographer, to illustrate it. Edward Sidney Caddick of Corfton in the Corvedale was an ideal candidate. Although Caddick was only a part time photographer and travelled a limited area, his work was extremely good and his subjects second to none. It has been difficult to compile this book for several reasons. Firstly, Caddick was a grocer who did a little photography as a sideline and this meant that only a limited number of picture postcards were available to use. Secondly, Caddick did not market his postcards the way larger photographers did and very often he would take 'one offs' for individuals, making the cards very rare. As Caddick often omitted to identify his postcards with his ESC initials on the front, it is possible that some of the pictures used in this book are not of his taking but care has been taken to try to identify them. Special thanks are due to Ted and Jean Weller from Hampshire who salvaged several glass plate pictures from Caddick's shed before its demolition.

It was decided to use an additional postcard publisher to help complete the pictorial history of the Corvedale, and the author has used Wilding of Shrewsbury who covered the Corvedale quite extensively. Wilding printed cards are not of real photographic quality but are still good quality. Thank you to Derek Walley, author of the Wilding's of Shrewsbury book, whose help has been invaluable. Thanks to the Shropshire Postcard Club (a friendly group which meets monthly at Bayston Hill Memorial Hall) for their various contributions and suggestions. Thanks to a local historian, Sam Hay, who lived in the Corvedale for thirty years, who passed on many snippits and anecdotes that he had collected over the years which would have been lost forever but for his forward thinking. Special thanks to Russell and Jeannette Jones of the Craven Arms History Group who have helped find useful information. Many thanks also to proof reader Vivienne Dodd. After compiling this book, the layout and text format was left to James Sherratt from Craven Design and Print in Craven Arms. He has worked extremely hard and has been very patient with the Author, changing text and adding pictures up until the very last day to print. Well done! Last but not least, thanks to the many locals who have given first hand information and photos of the area, especially Dick Edwards, the Beambridge blacksmith, Alan Brisbourne, Kath Woodhouse, Clive and Derek Crowther, Beatrice Millichap, Andrew Lane, Chris Jackson and Sheila Austin. Sincere apologies if anyone feels they have been left out.

Introduction

Before we move on to showing the Corvedale area, the author thought that the photographers should be introduced and, given that much of the book is their work, who could argue. We start with;

Edward Sidney Caddick.
Edward Sidney Caddick (or 'Sid' as he was known) was born in Retreat Street, Wolverhampton in 1901. He was the son of Edward and Martha Caddick. Sid's father, Edward, was a cabinet maker and moved the family into the Corvedale in the mid 1920's along with Sid's new wife, Edith Miriam Thrower. Miriam was the daughter of Mr and Mrs Thrower who kept the post office at Ludham in Norfolk. The picture below shows Miriam and Sid outside her parents' Post Office.

Ludham Post Office.

**The AJS sidecar erecting workshop
at Lower Walsall Street, Wolverhampton.**

Sid was manager at A. J. Stevens, the motorcycle manufacturers, where he made wireless set cabinets and motorcycle sidecars. He decided that he would start a new venture and purchased a Hillman 14 car to tow an Eccles van. This would be the beginning of a mobile shop, travelling around the Corvedale selling groceries and hardware.

It was not long before Sid had established a thriving business and secured a loyal core of customers. This persuaded Sid's father to purchase half an acre of ground from P.G. Holder, the land owner. The site was opposite their home, just across the Corvedale road. A timber bungalow and shop were erected for Sid and Miriam to move into. The stock from the mobile shop was transferred into their new shop and Caddick's Stores was created.

Sid was quick to take a photo of his new enterprise and again you can see his trademark ESC together with his caption, Corvedale Stores Corfton. The stock was expanded and anything the locals needed would be added to it. Candles, boots, paint, garden tools, clothes, wool, sweets, films and food of all descriptions. Alongside the shop they built a large garage (just to the left on the picture), where they stored the car and van together with a 50v Lister lighting plant which provided the shop and home with electricity. A section of the garage was used for charging wet batteries for customers' wireless sets leaving enough space for Sid to keep his hand in making the odd piece of furniture. At the back of the garage Sid partitioned a space off to use as a dark room to develop the films which he had become somewhat of an expert at taking. In the loft of the garage was a room where he would hold a slide projector show for the locals. Now the travelling shop was no longer needed, Sid converted it into a caravan and used it to tour all over. Towyn in North Wales was where they often frequented during the summer.

Miriam Caddick relaxing on the steps of her newly converted caravan during a journey to Towyn.

Business soon grew and staff were needed. Sheila Hodges worked for Caddick's for over thirty years and she became Mrs Eddie Austin, the well known proprietor of Austin's buses, that travelled the Corvedale as a regular service and also toured all over the country. In later years the fourteen year old son of Charlie Edwards the blacksmith, went to work at Caddick's. Pam Evans then worked as an assistant until her marriage to Denzil Lane.

Dick Edwards.

In the copy of a photo we can see Dick Edwards delivering a wet battery to a Caddick's customer. Dick was a keen young boy who quotes: "I was like a sponge, wanting to learn and take in any knowledge that would make me a better craftsman. It was 1939 when I went to work at Caddick's aged fourteen, earning eight shillings for a fifty hour week. I learnt everything; how to service the Lister engine, skin cheeses, make furniture, take photographs and develop films. They were very good to me at Caddick's and I stayed there until December 1942. Mr Caddick had died on August 28th, 1942, leaving £843.8s.3p, which was quite a lot in those days. I continued going out taking photos on his behalf until I joined up in the Army to do my bit in WW2. When I came out of the Army after the war in 1947, I went to work for the blacksmith, Fred Freeman, at Beambridge and took over the business in 1960, remaining there until my retirement in 1994". (Sadly Dick Edwards died in 2014, before this book went to the printers).

With the shop progressing and becoming profitable, Sid wanted to spend more time at his favourite hobby of photography. He was using a Thornton Pickard Reflex camera when he started taking pictures for his postcards but he wanted better and went off to buy a new camera. At a time when the Kodak Brownie camera was costing just five shillings, Sid bought a 1939 Contax camera at a cost of £87. It had a 1.5 Sonner lense and had a shutter speed of up to 1,200 parts of a second. It was capable of taking a picture of a dart in flight without any sign of a blur. Now he had the best gear, he could capture all the local houses and events in the Corvedale. His eye for a picture combined with his new super camera has given us a pictorial history of the Corvedale that can be cherished for years.

Wilding's of Shrewsbury.

The founder of Wilding's was Longworth Wilding, the son of a Manchester leather dealer, also named Longworth Wilding. Longworth junior was born on 29th April, 1850 and his mother was a Shropshire lass, Jane Owen, daughter of Thomas Owen the confectioner of Castle Street, Shrewsbury. Longworth left school to become a telegraphist at Shrewsbury Railway Station. He married Emily Susan Ellis from Wiltshire in 1874 and started his first business in 1875. He purchased the property and business of 33 Castle Street, Shrewsbury, a stationer, bookseller and printer, from Mr John Morris. As well as being busy running the printing business, Longford and Susan were blessed with two sons and two daughters between 1876 and 1881.

Longworth Wilding.

Business was good and, by 1895, they had ceased living above the shop and were living with their four children at a Georgian town house, 22 St John's Hill, Shrewsbury. It was in 1905 that Wilding's first produced their now famous picture postcards. A photograph would be taken and thousands of copies would be printed. All of Wilding picture postcards on sale were not real photographs but prints. Wilding's were printing the official guide of the Shrewsbury Corporation and started to use photographs and copper plates from the guide books. Using a lithographic process, the first vignette type cards were produced. The title, 'Salop Art Press', was added to the Wilding Shield Logo in 1893 and was used until 1910. Wilding's became a private limited company in 1910, with Longworth Wilding as managing director and son, William Owen Wilding, as manager. The founder's wife, Emily Susan Wilding died in 1915, followed by founder Longworth Wilding in 1918. William Owen Wilding then became managing director and faced the dilemma of getting Wilding's back into gear after the disruption that WW1 had caused. The shortage of paper supplies and employees being called up to serve in the First World War, had made the four year war period a very difficult time. Managing director, William Owen Wilding was joined by his son John Owen Wilding and they expanded and improved 'Wilding and Son Ltd., Printers and Publishers', throughout the 1920s and 1930s. Publishing books and booklets had become a large part of the business. The postcard side of the business had seen 600 individual cards produced in 1903 and up to 2400 by 1936. Depending on the popularity of the individual picture, on each postcard, indicated how many of each card should be printed.

It could be a 'one off' for a special occasion or thousands for a village scene. Despite the introduction of the telephone, which eventually did away with the need for postcard communication, Wilding's sold millions of cards during the boom years. The author, along with many other postcard collectors, are trying to collect the complete set of 2,400 Wilding postcards. WWII saw more difficult trading at Wilding's, not helped when William Owen Wilding died in 1942. His son John Owen Wilding took over the reins and continued to expand the printing and retail business. The author well remembers the days he spent at Shrewsbury Technical College 1953-1955, calling in to Wilding's Castle Street shop, to pick a record that would be played in a cubicle before he decided if he wanted to purchase it. By 1960, there were seventy employees at Wilding's and, although the postcard business had virtually finished, the printing of books and the retail business were still thriving up until 1965. Managing Director, John Owen Wilding, died suddenly whilst on a holiday cruise aged sixty two. Without a Wilding at the helm, the company declined and was sold to Stanley Sheridan Holdings. In 1973 the retailing business was sold off to a Birmingham based school suppliers, Midland Education Company. The printing works were sold in 1982, bringing an end to the Wilding printing business that had lasted for just over a century. What has been left behind is the postcard legacy that is keeping hundreds of collectors happy and thousands of Shropshire folk being able to see a pictorial history, in the form of Wilding picture postcards, for years to come.

Longworth Wilding's Windsor Place printing works of Shrewsbury in 1903.

Dawdling in the *Dale*

The author compiled this book, using the areas surrounding the river Corve, from its source at Spoonhill Wood near Bourton, continuing down the beautiful Corvedale valley for seventeen miles where it merges into the river Teme at Ludlow. The centre page map shows all the areas that are being described so that you can perhaps visit the places that interest you. To understand the once isolated area of the Corvedale, it is well to remember, that in 1300 it was part of the ancient Long Forest which stretched from Meole Brace to Sutton; along the line of the river Severn to Cressage and on to Much Wenlock; through the Corvedale to Craven Arms and then around the western side of the Longmynd and back to Meole Brace through Longden. The Head Forester's Lodge, dating from 1280, was situated at Upper Millichope and is the oldest domestic building in Shropshire.

The Foresters Lodge, Upper Millichope.

The head forester was there to protect the Royal hunting and game rights and to supply venison to the Priory of Much Wenlock. The forest laws of ancient times were so severe, in an effort to protect the game from the peasant classes, that a head forester's job was often dangerous. This explains why his house had to be a very secure and fortified place, having external walls six feet thick in places. It was in a poor state by the early C17 but it was later restored to its former glory and today it is a farmhouse.

Where better to begin our trip down the river Corve than at the source. The Corve rises on the north western side of Spoonhill Wood, off the Bourton to Monkhopton road (O.S. grid ref. 609959), in the form of two small springs under some moss covered stones, where it is little more than a puddle. The name Corvedale derives from the river Corve running through the dale. Originally it was named the river Culver, running through the Vale of Culverstone. Culverstone was one of the ancient Hundreds (1086), a defined boundary established in Anglo Saxon times. Later the Hundreds of Patton and Culverstone were combined and renamed the Hundred of Munslow. (Culvervale) then became Culverdale, finishing up as the present Corvedale. Situated near to the source is the stone built village of Bourton which is three miles south west of Much Wenlock.

Bourton Church.

Standing proudly at the top of the village, with views looking over Brown Clee Hill, Holy Trinity Church at Bourton, is surrounded by mature yew trees and was originally built in the C12 as a chapel to Much Wenlock. It has a weatherboard belfry with pyramid roof. The south doorway is Norman but much of the present church is of the 1844 restoration.

Bourton church pulpit.

The well carved Jacobean pulpit, lectern and reading desk are worth noting.

Bourton Manor.

East of the church is Bourton Manor. Bourton means settlement by a fortified manor and in 1086 the manor was held by Wenlock Priory. Edinburgh born Richard Norman Shaw (1831–1912) designed the present building, with its half timbered gable, stone arched doorway, sixteen brick chimneys and curiously irregular floor levels. Notable is the splendid ornate Jacobean staircase and the adjoining square, manorial dovecote built in similar style to the manor.

Bourton Village.

Bourton has shown its support for Royalty over the years. An avenue of chestnut trees were planted at the entrance to the village to commemorate the Diamond Jubilee of Queen Victoria and, for Queen Elizabeth's Coronation, a cherry tree was planted for each child in the village. The post office was kept by Mrs Tom Wall in 1904 and her husband was the blacksmith next door. Tom took on all tasks in ironwork such as working on Farley quarry kilns where lime was burnt for agriculture; also repairing farm implements and shoeing horses for half a century. Tom was a keen gardener and won prizes for his vegetables. Although he and his wife had busy working lives, they managed to bring up three sons and five daughters.

Bourton Village.

Bourton was on the main Much Wenlock, through the Corvedale to Ludlow road in the 13th century. In 1332 the road was named St. Mildburg Way. By 1736 it was called Bourton Lane and turnpiked in 1756 until disturnpiked in 1867. Through the ages Bourton has had much industry. Lime kilns, brick manufacturing, three tailors, cobbler, a mill since 1086, post office in 1870, The Talbot Pub 1841 until 1882. All gone!

Bourton National School.

There had been education provided at Bourton, in one form or another, since 1404. The last school, as shown above, was built by Lord Wenlock in 1901, replacing an earlier school. It consisted of brick and tile with the usual stamp and appearance of a rural Shropshire school, with seating for 112 pupils. Miss Beatrice Smith was Head Mistress at the school from 1918 until her retirement in 1957. In 1939, seventeen Liverpool evacuees and their teacher were admitted during WWII. With only fifteen pupils attending in 1967, it was decided to close the school and transfer them to Brockton and Much Wenlock schools.

Longville-in-the-Dale Railway Station.

A rival railway scheme from Dudley to Bridgnorth, through the Corvedale to Craven Arms was put forward by the Central Wales Railway and nearly scuppered plans for the proposed Much Wenlock to Craven Arms line. Talks were held to see if they could amalgamate but it was decided that it would not work. The picturesque Corvedale was saved and the Wenlock line went ahead with Dr. William Penny Brookes, the founder of the Wenlock Olympian Society as chairman. It finally opened to passengers on 16th December 1867. The line went from Much Wenlock, Westwood halt, Presthope, Easthope Halt, Longville station, Rushbury station, Harton Road, Marsh Farm Junction, Wistanstow Halt to Craven Arms, a 41 minute journey. Sadly at 5 o'clock on December 31st 1951 the last passenger train left Craven Arms to Much Wenlock. The end of an era after 84 years.

Easthope Church.

Although nearby Easthope is actually part of Hope valley, its locality comes within the river Corve area and the author has decided to include Hope Valley in this publication. Originally C12, the petite, Grade II listed, St Peters church at Easthope had a major restoration in 1852 on behalf of Moses George Benson of nearby Lutwyche Hall. A fire in 1928 gutted the church leaving just four walls, but it was rebuilt within a year. The wooden belfry was reinstated and the palisade altar rails were rescued and still remain.

Easthope Church interior.

The rare Saxon font is worth mentioning. A memorial window on the south side of the chancel is dedicated to Phillip Henry Riou Benson who was lost on the ship 'London' in the Bay of Biscay in 1866. In 1333 the Vicar, Will Germston, murdered the church's patron, John De Easthope and his ghost is said to haunt the churchyard.

Easthope Church bells.

In 1904 only three bells were at St Peters at Easthope but in 1920 Gillett and Johnston of Croydon recast them and added two more. One more was added in 1921 making it six. It has a carillon mechanism which has more in common with European tradition than that of English churches.

Easthope Hourglass.

On the south wall, next to the pulpit, is a rare wrought-iron hour-glass stand, dated 1662 and with the initials SS (Samuel Steadman, the incumbent). It is fixed to the wall by an iron bracket. Samuel was the rector from 1650 until 1672 and used the hourglass to measure the length of his sermons, half an hour in the summer and three quarters of an hour in winter.

Easthope Home Guard.

C. company (Corvedale) 7th Battalion of the Shropshire Home Guard under the command of Lieut.-Colonel J. I. Benson from Lutwyche Hall (extreme right) on Sunday church parade at Easthope in September 1940. The men were all from Easthope, Shipton, Brockton and Stanton Long. (Front far left) Sergeant Bert Davies was from Manor Farm Easthope. Harold South, the Brockton blacksmith is the middle man, 2nd row back. The Shropshire Home Guard 7th Battalion was formed in May 1940 and disbanded in December 1944.

Easthope Rectory.

The Easthope name goes back to the Old English origin meaning "dweller in the eastern region". The rectory at Easthope is Grade II listed and the original building was mentioned in 1291. Rev George Leon Gerold occupied the present C20 rectory for over two decades from 1901. Thirty six acres of glebe land were attached. The picture shows the present five bedroom rectory, built of stone and brick with a tiled roof. It was sold, freehold, in 2012 for £750,000.

Manor Farm, Easthope.

This building of the Easthope Manor dates from the C16 but an earlier building stood on the site. It was a hospice belonging to Wenlock Priory in the C13. During that period, two monks fought in the manor house kitchens, fell down some steps, killing both and they are buried beneath two yew trees in the churchyard. To save idle gossip no inscriptions were placed on their grave stones.

Easthope Mill.

The mill was mentioned in 1306 and could have been in existence well before. By 1891 the corn mill was driven by steam and water power, serving several nearby parishes.

Easthope Mill.

This picture shows Samuel and Thomas Philpott, owners of the mill in 1912. They were the children of Sara Acton and Samuel Philpott senior. Sara was the daughter of the well known Shropshire family, John and Mary Acton of nearby Larden. Thomas died in 1916 and Samuel in 1917. They left the mill to their nephew John Acton James Philpott who already owned the 204 acre farm at Upper House Brockton. He was master miller at Easthope Mill until its closure in 1926.

Stanway Manor.

Situated under Wenlock Edge in the very secluded Hope Valley, sitting just above the Corvedale is Stanway Manor. The Manor was built in brick by William Horton in 1836. He was a retired colliery owner and architect of Darlaston in Staffordshire.

Francis William Webb. (1836–1906)

From the early 1890's until 1903 Stanway Manor was occupied by F.W. Webb, a railway engineer from Crewe. He was responsible for the design and manufacture of locomotives for the London and North Western Railway (LNWR). He was also responsible for the remodelling of Crewe station which involved the building of four tracks in underpasses on the western side of the station to carry freight trains. He made numerous inventions and received over 80 patents. He was Vice-President of the Institute of Civil Engineers and the Institute of Mechanical Engineers. His salary was £3,000 in 1871 which shows the standard of his ability.

Lutwyche Hall.

Lutwyche Hall is situated three quarters of a mile south west of Easthope. It was built of brick in 1587, in an E shape, for Judge Edward Lutwyche. C16 finely decorated plaster ceilings are a main feature. Alterations in the C19 saw courtyards enclosed. The family lived there until 1776, selling to Moses Benson, a wealthy West India merchant and slave trader. The Benson family remained at Lutwyche until 1946. It later became a school but it is now a private residence.

Next comes the village of Brockton, named after the brook running through the village. It had been established as far back as 1086 and was later to have a motte and mill in 1256 and, much later, a pub, school and a dozen houses including a manor house.

The Feathers, Brockton.

At the crossroads in Brockton stands the C16 Feathers Pub. It was originally two Elizabethan cottages before their conversion into an inn. Over thirty original oak beams from the cottages are still in situ. One beam has an axe cut in it, put there when two local farm hands quarrelled in 1890. As a result, one was barred for life and the other carried a pint outside for his mate. The badge of the Prince of Wales was first adopted by the Black Prince (his arms were feathers) after he had killed John of Luxemburg at the battle of Crecy in 1346. John Cooper was the landlord in 1929 around the time this picture was taken.

Not far away from Brockton, high up on the hillside stands Larden Hall.

Larden Hall - Shropshire.
WILDING'S SERIES 727

Larden Hall.

This postcard of Larden Hall was posted in 1907 when the hall was in all its glory. It was originally built during the C16 for Thomas More, although part of the hall is thought to have been built in 1477 by his ancestor, William More. The date recorded over the front portal tells us that it was extensively added to in 1607 by Jasper More. Over the years it was altered, added to and, the amalgam of architectural styles and materials used, gives it quite a pleasing finish. Thomas More of Larden married Harriet Mytton from nearby Shipton Hall in 1795, bringing the two estates together with the birth of their son John. The Rouse Boughtons of Downton Hall near Ludlow, purchased the hall in 1859 and lived there for over thirty years. The More family bought it back again in 1894. Several tenants lived there until 1938 after which, Thomas Jasper Mytton More occupied it until it was sold in 1947.

Larden Hall Demolition.

In 1968 Larden Hall was demolished and transported to Dallas, Texas, America with thoughts of rebuilding it. Unfortunately that never materialised and it was used in several different buildings in America.

Larden Cottage.

Built by Thomas More, Larden Cottage, not to be confused with Larden Hall, was built around 1790 as a villa in the grounds adjoining Mogg Forest near to Larden Hall. In the early C19 the cottage grounds acquired a lake of two and a half acres formed by the construction of a massive dam on Brockton Brook. In 1926 the dam gave way and flooded some houses in Brockton. In 1966 the dam collapsed and the road in Brockton flooded to the depth of five feet which left thousands of eels to be gathered by the villagers. In 1988 Larden Cottage and pool were bought by a fishing syndicate who brought the lake back to its former glory.

Charles Green (1785–1870).

Although manned balloons were flying from 1784, it must have been quite a shock for the twelve farm workers at Skimblescott farm near Brockton, when Charles Green landed his coal-gas fired balloon in their clover field on August 26th, 1824. He had flown from Shrewsbury (about fourteen miles away), flying at 4,000 feet up, starting out at four in the afternoon and landing at 6.20 pm. He took along a pigeon to experiment with its flight from a high altitude. Mr More from nearby Larden Hall invited Charles home for supper and had a band playing music for him to celebrate his flight.

Balloonist, Charles Green.

Charles Green became one of the greats in ballooning, making 526 flights during his lifetime. In 1836 he flew four hundred and eighty miles from London to Germany in eighteen hours, accompanied by Monck Mason and sponsor, Robert Holland. That record was not broken until 1907. Charles planned, but never attempted, an Atlantic crossing. The small working model of his proposed balloon, flown in 1840, incorporated the first ever mechanically driven propeller to power an aircraft.

Down the B4378 for one mile is Shipton village, the name meaning 'sheep farm'.

Shipton Hall.

In 1587, Richard Lutwyche from Lutwyche Hall built Shipton Hall as a wedding present for his daughter Elizabeth, when she married a local landowner, Richard Mytton. The Hall was built on the previous site of a timber framed house that had been badly damaged by a fire. The whole of the old Shipton village was pulled down and removed a short distance further east, to leave splendid views from the new Hall windows for 'the newly weds'!

Shipton Hall stables with dovecote on the left.

A kitchen and library were added to Shipton Hall in 1760. As was a Georgian stable block with central entrance arch, topped by a cupola. Close to the stable is a restored C13 dovecote. Young doves, called 'squabs', were removed from the pigeon holes around the external walls by a young lad called a 'least lad' retained to do the various jobs around the farm. There is a tunnel from Shipton that leads to the fireplace in Larden Hall, a mile away. The Mytton family lived at Shipton Hall for three hundred years until 1872 when it passed to the More's of nearby Larden Hall. At the turn of the century a relative on the female side of the family married Charles Bishop and the descendants of that family are still in residence to this day.

Shipton Church.

In the grounds of Shipton Hall is the small stone built church of St James that dates back to Saxon times, first mentioned in 1110. The Norman nave and chancel were restored in 1589 by John Lutwyche of Lutwyche Hall. The squat west tower with pyramid roof is from the C12. The interior of the church had a major restoration in 1955.

River Corve.

The river Corve is still nothing more than a gutter with a little water running down the dale at Shipton. Who would think that this drop of water could eventually become a fully fledged river capable of sweeping away bridges as it did at Ludlow in 2007.

Crossing over the River Corve seven miles from Much Wenlock, is the village of Stanton Long or Long Staunton as it was once known, Only three inhabitants lived there in 1086. In 1845 there was a church, vicarage, ten cottages, four farmhouses, a blacksmith and a wheelwright. Originally the hamlet was Staunton but the Normans, in the C12, seeing that it was a strung out hamlet, added "Long" to avoid confusion with another nearby Stanton.

Stanton Long Vicarage.

The Rev Alfred Ernest Ball and his wife look across the lawn towards their children at the Stanton Long vicarage in 1909. The vicarage had sixty six acres of glebe land attached to it. The back of the postcard tells us that this photo was taken to sell at their sale to raise money for the church.

Stanton Long Church.

St Michaels and All Angels church at Stanton Long, dates from the C12. Renovation was carried out in 1842 and in 1870 costing £400. The weather boarded belfry has a pyramid roof and contains three bells which were recast in 1893 at a cost of £61. The clock was given by the Wadlow family in 1927. The impressive C12 main entrance door has attractive iron scrollwork, an iron ring to close the door and hooks for a notice board.

Just a short distance away to the west is the village of Holdgate.

Holdgate Church.

Holy Trinity church at Holdgate is situated in an elevated position overlooking the Trow Brook and river Corve. It is situated in the south west bailey of what was Holdgate Castle. The nave is Norman but the chancel and west tower are C13. A school room was partitioned off in the church after 1793. A Victorian entrance porch covers a splendid Norman doorway. High on the south wall, adjacent to the chancel window, is a Sheela-na-gig, a pagan fertility figure. Young ladies believed that placing themselves before the carved figure would result in their pregnancy. In 1854 and again in 1894 the tower was rebuilt, a new roof was reconstructed on the nave and the chancel.

Holdgate was known in Saxon times as Stanton and the present name is a corruption of Helgot, a Norman baron who owned the surrounding lands. Helgot's castle is recorded in the Doomsday Book. The motte of the castle is at the edge of the churchyard. Beyond this site, to the right of a track, is a predominantly C18 farmhouse, Set into the back of the house is part of the stone tower of a later castle built in 1280 by Robert Burnell. Henry I visited Holdgate castle in 1109 and, his viceroy, Richard de Belmeis, held a great court there in 1115. In the reign of Richard I it passed to the Maudits of Warminster, collateral heirs to the barony. In Henry III's time they sold it to the King's brother, Richard Plantagenet, who installed the Knights Templar there for a season but afterwards sold it to Robert Burnell, Bishop of Bath and Wells, the Great Chancellor of England. It remained in his family until the Barony fell into abeyance. Just across the road from the castle are the grassy shapes which mark the site of a medieval village. Holdgate castle was garrisoned for the king in the Civil War but it was abandoned and rendered incapable of defence on the fall of Shrewsbury in 1645. Holdgate was a place of great importance in the early days and a weekly market, to be held on a Thursday, was granted in 1222.

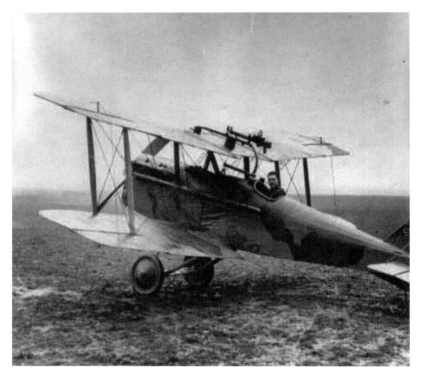

1918 aeroplane tragedy at Hungerford.

At 11am on 27th June 1918, Arthur Davies, a flight cadet in the RAF, who had been flying for only six weeks, developed engine trouble in his 80hp plane and was forced to land in a field at Hungerford. He landed perfectly but damaged the plane's under carriage when he hit a bush. Although Hungerford was in the countryside, there was soon a gathering of some thirty people standing around the plane. The pilot soon found that a faulty carburettor was the problem and he asked bystander, Samuel James of Stanton Lacy, to help with the propeller while he tried to start the engine. As it was only an 80hp engine and the throttle was only halfway out, the pilot thought that if it did start, the plane would not move forward, so no one held the tail of the plane and no one was in the plane. After ten minutes the engine started and the plane quickly spun around to the left, narrowly missing the pilot who was stood at the side. There was a scream. A young boy crawled out unhurt from under the plane but, unfortunately, his 18 year old sister, Harriet Bounds, daughter of Edward Bounds of Rowe Lane, Stanton Long had been struck by the propeller and was killed instantly. John Allen from Holdgate Hall Farm had seen the plane come down into his field and joined the onlookers to see if he could help. He sent Thomas Jukes, the rural postman from 24 Market Street, Craven Arms, to get a doctor and a policeman to the scene. At a later inquest, the Coroner suggested standing further back from such incidents and returned a verdict of accidental death.

Holdgate Rectory.

This large, brick built rectory with gothic details, by J.P. Seddon, was built near to the church in 1865. It included 86 acres of glebe land and the resident rector (Curate in charge) in 1909, at the time of this picture, was Rev Russell Henry Jeffrey. The Rectory was sold in 1959 and renamed Holdgate House. The bishop bought land for a new parsonage in 1963 but the project failed to reach fruition. A little way down the road is the Thonglands.

The Thonglands.

Known as Tangelanda in 1126, the township of Thonglands is mentioned in the Doomsday book and was in Tugford parish. It was a separate parish until its union with Munslow. The principle residence of the township has a well moated, Grade II listed, half timbered house that was built by the De Bradeley family on the ruins of a C13 chapel. Nearby is part of an ancient tomb that marks the site of a grave yard. In 1700 the timber framed hall was encased in stone and completely altering the appearance of the house. A dovecote stood adjacent to the hall to provide food. Trow Brook flows south west into the river Corve near Thonglands. In 1863, Mrs Ann Edwards was the publican of 'The Butchers Arms' at the bottom of Primrose Bank. It was frequented by colliers and quarrymen who worked on Clee Liberty, but who lived in the Munslow area and so walked by it every day, to and from work. It was referred to by them as the 'Drum and Monkey'. It first opened in 1851 and closed in 1920. A Primitive Methodist Chapel opened nearby in 1861 and closed in 1963. On down the road, heading west, you will come to Tugford.

Tugford Church.

Ten miles south west of Much Wenlock, on the lower slopes of Brown Clee Hill, is Tugford brook. Nearby, St Catherine's church at Tugford, was originally built around a village green. Early in the C17, squatters built cottages on the green in front of the church but were ordered to remove them by the Manor Court. Tugford had its own village hall up until the mid 1940's, situated on the bridleway to the Heath but it was pulled down just after WWII. The Norman church has a C12 nave, C14 chancel and tower. High up and one on each side of the south door, are two pagan fertility sheela-na-gigs - only four exist in the whole of Shropshire. The five bells are dated 1636-95. The windows have clear glass and inside the church are box pews and a gallery. The church band was discontinued in 1869 and choir stalls were installed. The nearby rectory was built in the C16 and it was sold in 1930, along with seventeen acres of glebe land. A chapel in 'Tugaford' is mentioned in 1138 but no longer exists.

Sheep Dipping at Tugford.

The majority of Tugford men were employed in farming. 'Warin of Tugford' was the very first Sheriff of Shropshire, sometime prior to 1066.

Looking east from Tugford, you will see the western slopes of the Brown Clee Hills, where the township of Abdon is perched. In 1760 Abdon was the site of charcoal furnaces which gave rise to the road name 'Furnace Bank', although, by this time, the wooded area around Tugford had shrunk to less than 100 acres.

Abdon Church.

Abdon's St Margaret's church dates back to 1138 and it stands on a circular mound which was the site of a deserted medieval village from the C14. The township's original name was 'Abetune' meaning 'Abba's tun', or the 'settlement of Abba'. The churchyard is circular which probably indicates a pre-Christian site. The church has a compact nave and chancel, with a western double bellcote. Inside there is a primitive 700 year old timber construction between the nave and chancel, with two upright posts against the lateral walls, two inner posts and, linking them transversely, a tie beam with a king post and diagonal queen posts. Thus they form a tripartite entrance. Seating is provided for a congregation of 100 people.

Abdon Clee Stone Quarry Works.

Abdon Clee Quarry.

Rising to 1755 feet above Abdon is Abdon Burf – the highest hill in Shropshire. It was 1806 feet high until quarrying took its toll. At its summit are the remains of an oval shaped Iron Age enclosure, covering about thirty acres. Its earthen walls were sixty five feet wide at the base, but, again, quarrying has obliterated much of it. In the C16, coal was mined here and taken to Ludlow Castle by pack-horse. Just prior to WW1 the Abdon Quarry Stone Company brought out an 'Asphalt Carpet' consisting of broken stone and tar. A gas engine drove the stone crusher and the gas was produced from anthracite in the nearby gas plant. Quarrying of Dolerite, known locally as 'dhustone', had been active at Abdon Burf from 1908 until 1936. Dhustone is a hard, black rock that is used for road making and stone setts. The Abdon setts were preferable to the nearby Titterstone Clee setts because they did not polish and become slippery.

Abdon Clee Quarry.

Quarry workers would walk to the quarry from as far away as Ludlow and Bridgnorth. They would wield a twenty eight pound hammer to break the stone working twelve hours a day. Horses were used to haul the stone down to Ditton Priors and to take the empty trucks back up the hill.

Abdon Quarry Locomotive.

Abdon Quarry light railway was established to carry the stone down to Ditton Priors from the quarry, relieving some of the work of the horses.

Abdon Incline.

An 800 feet inclined plane was erected for the railway to carry the stone down the hill. The rails would be moved and re-laid regularly as each section of quarry face was worked out. In 1908, Ben Revell was fatally injured when the engine he was driving, coupled to another driven by Jack Strong were pushing trucks up the 1 in 13 rise and lost power. Both engines slid back down the incline. Ben Revell fell from his footplate and the other engine ran over him. In 1919, three, petrol driven, Simplex ex WD locomotives, were acquired to work from the quarry face. They were nicknamed 'whizz bangs' because of their habit of back firing. Whilst the rest of the country was feeling the effects of 'the depression' in 1926, trade increased at the quarry. The stone crushing and tarmac plant were flat out and the concrete works at Ditton Priors were busy making prefabricated buildings of cement and powdered dhustone. This was a 'quick fix solution' to the housing problem which hit the country after WW1. At its peak, two hundred men worked at the stone cutting and crushing works enduring terrible working conditions but the main production of tramway setts declined in the 1920s. In 1921 the second fatality occurred. Wilfred Morris was killed whilst handling wagons when a runaway wagon crushed him.

Foster Steam Wagon used at Clee Hill.

Throughout the 1920s and 30s, the Dhustone deposits were diminishing and the work force went down to twenty. In 1937, the 'breakers' – Simms Lewis of Sheffield – started to dismantle the quarry equipment. Whilst they were cutting up the old drum from the incline, a low flying RAF plane flew over them in a dense fog and they heard it crash at Stanton Long, killing all members of the crew.

Clee Hill Road Gang.

This postcard shows the Clee Hill road gang using stone from Abdon Quarry to mend the road at Caynham. The last big order was received in 1938 for stone to lay the new Church Stretton by-pass. WWII led to the enlistment of most of the workforce. The concrete works were kept busy for a while but, after Bryants of Birmingham built the Royal Navy Armaments Depot at Ditton Priors in 1941, the concrete works closed. The tarmac plant closed in 1942. The Brown Clee industrial era was over and the area could now go back to sleep. Well remembered names at the quarry were, quarry manager, Hamish Cross and engine drivers, Charlie Harris, Horace Hodnet and Harold Bradley. James Ritchie was quarry foreman and his assistant was Doug Morris. Jack Green was in charge of the crusher feeder and Charlie Cooper the crusher. The foreman of the gas plant works was Bill Hodnet. The horses were looked after by Job James, Will Mountain and Bert Cartwright.

Norncott.

Lower and Upper Norncott have both been included in the Heath civil parish since 1884. Upper and Lower Norncott farms are three quarters of a mile apart and date back to the C17. Earthworks between them indicate the site of a deserted hamlet from an earlier date. Norncott was part of Stoke St Milborough Manor in 1086. Enclosure of open field arable land for pasture was reported at Norncott in 1517.

The Norgrove family came to Lower Norncott in 1921 and remained there until 1992. Here we see the Norgrove family: Thomas, Hilda, Mary, Thomas, Rosa, Arthur, Emma and Anne. Anne, the young girl on the right became the mother of Ray, Douglas and Mary Heighway of Clee St Margaret. Upper Norncott was owned by the Bradley family from 1913 until 1992.

River Corve.
The Corve is now developing into a river, gathering speed and beginning to widen.

Beambridge.

Taking the lane down from Abdon and approaching the B4368 Corvedale Road is Beambridge. The building on the far left is the laundry for Millichope Hall. The fisherman is having a sandwich and watching the world go by, looking over the river Corve in Beambridge. The view would have been very different if the Shropshire Mineral Railway had been given the go ahead. In 1845 Samuel Clegg surveyed and planned the railway which would have run from Craven Arms to Much Wenlock, north of the river Corve, passing between the beam bridge over the river Corve and the blacksmith's shop. In the 1930's, County Council Records Office looked at it again but, as in 1845, the funding was not forthcoming. The detailed plans and maps are still in the Shropshire Council Records Office.

Blacksmiths Shop at Beambridge.

Coming out to the B4368 junction, on the right is the blacksmiths shop at Beambridge. The signpost at the side of the road is situated where the Wenlock toll keeper's cottage once stood. It was established in 1756 and demolished at the end of the C19. The Millichope Bridge, nearby to the west, has a stone that marks the exact boundaries between the Ludlow toll system and Wenlock toll system.

Blacksmiths Shop, Beambridge.

Tom Wall was the blacksmith at Beambridge in 1891. In 1912, Fred Freeman took over, moving from his Bouldon forge. A young Charles Edwards, born in Westhope in 1900, was taken on as an apprentice at the age of fourteen, coming straight from school. In 1948 Charles left the employ of Fred Freeman and set up his own business from the smithy at Corfton Hall. He was a first class farrier and worked regularly for Hyde's racing stables at nearby Lawton. In the picture we can see young apprentice Charles Edwards wielding a hammer, about to give the plough a 'straightening up'. Fred Freeman Senior is on the right holding the plough handles.

Dick Edwards and wife Phyllis sitting on the new memorial seat.

Charles retired at the age of seventy and enjoyed twenty two years retirement before dying in 1992 - aged ninety two. Charles's son Dick made a seat as a memorial to his father and placed it in Munslow square. Dick Edwards, on leaving the army after the war, went to work for Fred Freeman at Beambridge. In 1960 Fred Freeman offered him the opportunity to take over Beambridge forge, which he did. He became renowned for his entrepreneurial skills and ideas when tackling various jobs in metalwork. No job was too big or too small for him. He retired in 1994. After helping the author with facts about the Corvedale, Dick sadly passed away in 2014.

New and old Millichope Hall.

Millichope Park, on the formerly named Lower Millichope estate, stands high up on the north side of Broadstone and is Grade II listed. The estate was once owned by Roger de Montgomery but he later exchanged it for the Eardington estate belonging to the monks of Wenlock. The More family of Bishops Castle bought the estate in 1544. The old black and white timber framed and plaster hall was built by the More family in the late C16. The New house, built in 1839, costing £30,000 was built of Grinshill stone. It was designed by Edward Haycock of Shrewsbury for Revd. Robert Norgrave Pemberton who had inherited the estate in 1832. The old house was demolished in 1842.

Millichope Hall Rotunda.

Extensive gardens and deer parkland were introduced in 1760 including a rotunda which was built as a memorial to Thomas More's two sons. Leighton More died at sea on board the Royal Navy's 'Burford' man of war in 1744 aged 24. John More was a Major in the 79th regiment and he was slain at the storming of the city of Manilla in 1762 aged 42. The specimen trees in the park include a 98ft high Lawson Cypress which was claimed to be the tallest in Shropshire and a 125ft high redwood with a girth of nearly 24ft. The last of the More family, Katherine who had married her cousin, Robert More of More left the estate to her cousin Robert Pemberton. He died in 1794 and left the estate to Thomas Pemberton who left it to his nephew, the Rev Robert Norgrave Pemberton in 1832. He was Rector of Church Stretton in 1818.

New Millichope Hall.
The Pemberton family sold Millichope Park in 1896 to Captain Henry John Beckwith, ancestor of the present owner.

Millichope Hall.
From 1943 to 1947, nuns ran an evacuated Roman Catholic girls school at Millichope Park. Until 1962 it was used as a boys boarding school and it then reverted back to a private residence.

Back at Beambridge - follow the B4368 eastwards towards the hamlet of Broadstone where, in 1929, Samuel Brown kept the Seven Stars pub; John Clinton was the local carpenter; Sara Edwards kept the shop; Arthur Nash was milling at the mill and Sidney Edwards was at Broadstone farm.

Seven Stars, Broadstone.

The Seven Stars at Broadstone was once named Field Hall House malthouse. The Seven Stars is a religious sign representing the seven starred, celestial crown which the Virgin Mary was usually shown wearing. The pub has been situated on the side of the B4368 since 1840 when Thomas Cocks was the first landlord. It had stabling for four horses and four bedrooms. In 1902 it was owned by the now defunct Ludlow and Craven Arms Brewery Company.

Ted Bridgwater.

One of the regulars at the Seven Stars was Ted Bridgwater from Abdon. He was born in 1904 and went to work mainly at New House farm Shipton. Ted was also a rabbit catcher and became a real character. He would push his ladies bicycle festooned with rabbits whilst accompanied by Rover, his lurcher dog. He claimed not only to have seen the ghost of the Buck's Head but also to have heard the ghost choir of Thonglands.

Rabbit was a common meal in the Corvedale, especially in wartime, when meat was on ration. Unfortunately the disease, mixamatosis, wiped out the rabbit population for several years.

Broadstone Mill.

Formerly named "Upper Mill", Broadstone Mill sits down below the Seven Stars on the river Corve. It was built by William Hazeldine for Richard Grant in 1794 at a cost of £350. William Hazeldine was a friend of Thomas Telford and they worked together on several projects. Hazeldine cast the iron frame for the Ditherington Flax Mill in Shrewsbury, being the first iron framed building in the world. In 1885, W.Morris, the tenant of Broadstone mill, wrote complaining that nothing had been done to the road which ran from the Seven Stars to the Ludlow to Bridgnorth turnpike road, past Broadstone Mill to Holdgate, since February, 1883. (thoughts; "nothing changes"). In 1924, Hiram Priest waded through flood water to cut a notch in the mill door to show the height of the flood. The mill closed in the 1930's. Broadstone was the home of the district nurse, Betsy Lancet. In 1929, she cycled throughout the Corvedale, bringing babies into the world and treating the sick. She later married Leonard Childes the gardener at Millichope Park. Broadstone Stores was accessible at the side of the B4368 and sold everything the local population needed. Mrs Sara Edwards was the proprietor in 1929 and Mr and Mrs Van Dyke were the last shopkeepers there. They retired to Ludlow in 1985.

Arthur Woodhouse and son Bill mowing at Upper House Farm in 1954.

Arthur Woodhouse came to Upper House Farm at Middlehope in 1947, followed by his son Bill in 1981.

Broadstone Church.

Broadstone church is located in an isolated spot between the Corvedale and Holdgate road. It was built as an agricultural building and 'chapel of ease' to Munslow, in the C17, with bi-annual church services held there until the 1843 restoration. It has a Victorian bell-turret on the eastern side and the roof comprises of tie-beams and queen posts. The small, carved pulpit dates from the C17 and the building is now Grade II listed.

To the north, high up on the hillside, is the medieval hamlet of Middlehope. It is a very secluded and picturesque part of the Hope Valley. The C12 earthwork castle has now disappeared and the hamlet consists of a scattering of old farmhouses that are noteworthy for their massive, stepped chimneys jutting out from gables.

Hall Farm, Middlehope.

Hall Farm house is a C17, timber framed building that replaced an earlier house. Thomas Child and his descendants farmed here from 1605 until 1702. Ernest Yapp was the tenant in 1914 and in 1964 Bill and Kathleen Woodhouse farmed there. It is now a private residence and since 1985, has been the home of Martin and Megan Speight. Martin is an author and founder member of the Ludlow Historical Research Group.

Lower House Farm, Middlehope.

The Wellen family lived on the 165 acre Lower House farm, Middlehope for nearly a century after 1605. They were followed in 1671 by the vicar of Acton Scott and Diddlebury, the revd. William Fosbrooke who leased the farm and sublet it to the Wellen family until 1712. William was imprisoned in Hereford gaol for praying for the King during the Commonwealth ascendancy. William sublet the farm to his own son Thomas in 1713. It stayed with the Fosbrooke family until 1830 and a year later the new tenant was John Yapp. The Yapp family lived there until David Yapp purchased the farm from the Millichope Estate in 1995 and then sold it to Mark and Fiona Jarrold in 1999.

Upper House Farm, Middlehope.

The largest farm in Middlehope is the C16, two storied, Upper House Farm which is an attractive timber framed building. John Downe was the occupant in 1575 followed by John Baldwyn, son of the Squire of Diddlebury, his descendants were tenants from 1670 until 1725. In 1981, Bill and Kathleen Woodhouse moved from Hall Farm, Middlehope to Upper House Farm and they became its owners in 1995 when the Millichope estate was sold off.

Middlehope Landslide.

In 1947, thirty metres of the hillside high above Middlehope slid downhill, taking hedges and a tree and leaving the road completely blocked. In the photograph, Mr Arthur Davies from Green Farm inspects the damage.

Green Farm, Middlehope.

Green Farm is a C17 timber framed farmhouse which had a large, brick built wing, added to it in the C19. In 1713 the annual rent was £4 a year. In 1913 it was valued at £790 with its 80 acres of land. Stanley Carter from Burwood was the tenant in 1955 and he was followed by his son Michael. The house was separated from the ground in 1995 when the Millichope estate was sold off.

Fernolds Mill.

The Georgian farmhouse, which was named 'Fernalls Mill', (although Caddick's caption has it as 'Fernolds Mill'),was built just above the original cruck–framed mill that stood on the banks of the Bache Brook and Thomas Fernalls lived here in the C17. The old mill was used as two cottages up until the end of WWII but it became derelict and collapsed in the late 1960s. Fernalls Mill farmhouse was separated from the farmland when Frederick Corfield died and it is now a private residence.

Wetmore Farm, Middlehope.

At the north eastern end of Middlehope stands Wetmore Farm and here an Edward Lewis farmed in 1661. The farm was purchased by the Millichope estate in 1913 and rented out to Ernest Ray in 1926. Diddle Brook rises at Wetmore and runs through Middlehope, across Dunstans Lane, leaving Hopedale to enter the Corvedale just before Bache Mill. After passing through Diddlebury it enters the river Corve between Lawton and Sparchford.

Munslow Village.

On down the B4368 is Munslow, which is one of the largest villages in the Corvedale. Probably named after Mundel's burial mound, Munslow was first mentioned in the C12 and was originally less important than Aston Munslow, one mile away.

This Caddick postcard shows Munslow in 1905 and one of the village shops on the left was a butcher's shop with slaughterhouse. At the eastern end of the village was another butcher's shop and slaughterhouse built by Charles Farrington in 1920 which became the business of a well liked butcher, Charlie Pryce, in more recent times. His father had been the bailiff at Delbury Hall. Charlie retired to Diddlebury and later to Ludlow in 1994. The last butcher operating here was Brian Bell, closing in 1984. The Post Office and Shop by the kiosk were kept by sub post mistress Mrs Emma Bishton. Edward Evans was postmaster in 1895 as well as being a draper, tailor and 'registrar of births and deaths' for the area. After moving several times, the post office was closed in 1997 and transferred to Aston Munslow garage. Hemp was a lucrative crop to grow as it was used for making rope and coarse linen and it was grown extensively in the Corvedale. The hempyard in Munslow was immediately to the west of Munslow farm. Hemp would not dry quickly enough in our climate so the workers dug a hole and lit a fire in it. The hemp was then suspended over this "gig pit" until it was dry. By 1825, foreign competition and manmade fibres, led to the lack of demand for hemp and the demise of the hemp industry in the Corvedale.

Much of the village of Munslow is situated off the B4368. The road up to the church is worth exploring with its massive, stone houses built high on a rock face. The house now named "The Coach House" was once the Munslow Working Men's clubroom which opened in the late 1800s and closed in the 1930s. Also in the 1930s, during the winter months, a mobile cinema was set up in a tent erected on Townsend field opposite Clee View and adjacent to Churley Way. The Sharratt family charged 1p for children and 3p for adults. There, schoolboy Eddie Austin of Aston Munslow saw his first talking movie starring Al Jolson. Munslow had two horse race courses from 1807, both situated just north of Churley Bridge which crosses the river Corve on the Churley Way. This enabled the organisers to 'rest' one course long enough for the surface to recover between race meetings. Race day at Munslow was a great day out with entertainment for everyone. There would be fairground rides, stalls, cockfighting, pig catching, boxing booths and of course horse racing. On Tuesday 9th January 1851, steward James Beddoes, presided over one of the best day's sport ever seen at Munslow. Well behaved gentlemen of Ludlow, Wenlock, Bridgnorth, Shrewsbury and surrounding neighbourhoods were present. The Corvedale Stakes, with a value of one sovereign each with £5 added was won by the favourite, Mr Langley's 'Shamlass', ridden by his jockey Edwards. Most of the company of people retired to Mr Cadwallader's Hundred House to dine whilst the remainder stayed upon the course to enjoy more rural sport. The dinner gave great satisfaction, reflecting much credit on the host and hostess. James Beddoes was in the chair and gave the usual toasts, which were responded to. The health of various gentlemen was drunk to. The chairman then rose to propose Mr Richard Bache of Medley Park be the steward for next year.

On 12th August 1854, a great many sporting gentlemen favoured this meeting with their presence, some coming from a great distance. The sport was good as there were some crack nags on the ground. After the morning race the company returned to the Crown Hotel, where a splendid dinner for about 50 was provided; the dinner and wine gave general satisfaction and Richard Whiteman presided. The running commenced with the Corvedale Hurdles Race of 10s each, with 7 sovereigns added, over four flights of hurdles. Mr Turley's 5 year old, The Deformed, came first.

This cup clearly shows that it was won on October 18th 1836 at Munslow Races. The other side of the cup shows a racehorse and jockey. The owner of the winning horse that year was Samuel Bluck ,1781–1866, who bred pedigree cattle and sheep at Bromfield House, Bromfield. His grandson emigrated to Australia where the cup is still in the hands of his descendants. No record of when Munslow races ceased has been found, but by 1880 only Ludlow survived out of all the Shropshire race courses and that it is still operating today.

Munslow Garage.

The proprietor of Munslow Garage, Mr Edmunds, can be seen next to the petrol pump and mechanic, Bob Edwards, by the car at Munslow garage in the 1960s. The garage is next door to the Crown Inn.

Munslow Church.

The C12 St Michael's church at Munslow is situated in a small wooded hollow and is built of Aymestry limestone. It has a Norman tower, topped with a C18 parapet. The wooden porch is C14 and the stained glass windows are at least 500 years old. Many additions and restorations have taken place at various times, with repairs in 1815 and 1841. Inside St Michael's there are several memorials. There are wall monuments made of slate to William Churchman of nearby Holloway, dated 1602, to Richard Baldwin de Munslow dated 1689 and to Thomas More of nearby Millichope, dated 1767. A large brick from the Great Wall of China, brought to the church in 1884 and a wall plaque to Edward Stedman, 'Gent of Aston', dated 1777 can also be seen.

An epitaph in the cemetery reads: Goodbye dear friends and children dear,
I've lived with you for many a year.
I've always tried to do my best,
But now I've gone to take a rest.

Near the church stands the Miller House where Ormerod Edward Booth lived in 1891. He was 'a surgeon, Medical Officer and Public Vaccinator'.

Munslow Rectory - Shropshire.

Munslow Rectory.

There has been a rector in Munslow since 1115 but the splendid Munslow Rectory, west of the church, was built in 1793. Two pairs of Ionic pillars at the entrance, show off the three storey, elegant building surrounded by its 125 acres of glebe land. Rev George Bather Powell was rector in 1905 when this photo was taken. The Powell family were Rectors at Munslow from 1776 until 1965. Not all went well for the Rectors during their stay at Munslow and some were excluded for 'wrong doings'. Rev Ellis was murdered in 1298 and Rev Walter Lawrence (1418-22) resigned after being castrated! This Rectory was sold in 1967 and replaced by a rectory in Park Lane. The old Rectory was renamed Munslow House in the 1980s.

MUNSLOW RECRUITS 1-9-1914

Munslow Recruits 1914.

This postcard shows us the Munslow recruits on the 1st of September, 1914. These young men went off to WW1 at the very beginning. Third from left in the back row is Fred Preece who, after the war, became the Craven Arms saddler in Corvedale Road. The little boy in the front is Frank James Lindsay Bury from Millichope Hall. He became a Lt. 4 Commando, Royal Norfolk Regiment in WWII. Sadly he was killed during the Normandy landings on 11th July 1944, aged 33.

Ernest and Annie Ray.

This photo was taken on their wedding day in 1926, at Wetmore Farm on the Millichope estate. Ernest is in the picture of the Munslow recruits, (fourth from left on the back row) and served throughout WWI before settling down. Mrs Ray died in 1993 aged 97 and her son Dennis and daughter Dorothy farmed Wetmore until Dennis's death in 2002.

The War Memorial, Munslow.

Munslow War Memorial.

A war memorial stands in front of the old school with the names of nine of the fallen in WW1 and three of the fallen of WWII. The Munslow and Tugford War Veterans Fund was set up in 1921 to show appreciation to the Munslow volunteers of WWI which was to run until at least 1988 or until all the beneficiaries had died. In 1997 the trust was closed and the remaining funds were given to the Corvedale women's and men's British Legion.

Munslow School.

When this postcard was sent in 1917, Oates Hocking Thomas was the headmaster at Munslow school and he can be seen holding his son on the wall in the centre of the picture. Rev Roger Stedman ran a school in Munslow in 1573 and a Dame school was operating in the C18. Munslow school was built as a private house in 1658 for John Baldwin and his wife Abigail. Edward Littleton was born here and baptised in Munslow Church on March 15th 1589. He went on to become Solicitor General and was knighted on June 6th, 1635. On 18th February 1640 he was created a Baronet and became the 1st Lord Littleton, Baron of Munslow and keeper of the Great Seal to Charles 1st. He died on August 27th 1645 and was buried at Christ Church Oxford. Our picture shows us Munslow Manor House, renamed later as Munslow School and in 1849 it became the National School of the day. The entry for September 5th 1870 read, "Working school very dull, most of class 1 absent. Children engaged in pulling linen to pieces to make lint for wounded soldiers". In 1872 a new schoolroom was added. There were 55 children attending in 1922. Set in the boundary wall of the old school are the remains of a public tap that is surrounded by rather ornate stonework and bears the inscription "VR 1837-1887" which indicates that it was installed to commemorate the Golden Jubilee of Queen Victoria. Health and safety fears led to the tap being disconnected in the 1950s. In 1982, with only 29 children attending, the school was closed and was sold to provide a private house once again.

"I would rather trust a woman's instinct than a man's reason"

Stanley Baldwin

Crown Hotel, Munslow.

Standing proud on the side of the B4368 in Munslow, is the old Hundred House where once medieval manorial Court Leets were held. Later renamed Munslow Inn, it is presently called The Crown Inn. The building that we see today, is of mid C18 construction, but it has been much altered and covers many periods. It now has Grade II listing. There are traces of very early timber framing at the rear of the property. The first public licence was granted in 1790. In 1841 the landlord was William Wigmore and in 1891, Joseph Brown. The Brown family sold the Inn but retained the attached Crown farm, which was renamed Clee View farm. In 1978, Joseph Brown's grandson, Harold J Brown, sold the farm with its 160 acres and buildings. John Preece, a local character, lived in a caravan at the rear of the Crown and he spent his retirement walking up and down Munslow Bank. He died in 1995 and was buried in Munslow after the locals had a 'whip-round' to pay for his funeral. The Crown is currently run by Richard and Jane Arnold and is renowned for its excellent food and cosy B&B.

Mr Hodges, the postman with post lady, Mrs Evans.

Opposite the Crown Hotel, where the BT substation now stands, was the postman's hut. It was a wooden hut, containing desk, chairs, bunk and a solid fuel stove. The postman or post lady would be dropped off from Craven Arms, deliver the mail and would then rest in the hut until it was time to collect the mail from the post boxes. The mail van would then pick the post and postman up and return them to base at Craven Arms.

Munslow dominoes team showing off their spoils at the Crown Inn. Dennis Round, standing far right was a 'barnado boy' who came to the Corvedale in his early teens from a home in Ludlow to work as a farm labourer. Dennis worked for many years for Frank Davis at Lower House farm, Aston Munslow. He became a well liked character in the Corvedale, walking the river, watching mink, moorhens, dippers and kingfishers nesting. He loved hunting with the beagles and knew the area as well as anyone and therefore, a walk with Dennis was a walk with Mother Nature. He spent his last days in a flat at Hungerford Mill and was buried in the Green Cemetery at Westhope. A hard wood bench, paid for by the locals, was erected on the village green in his memory and a brass plaque notes the dates 1937 – 1997.

Hungerford Mill.

Hungerford Mill, Grade II listed, was originally the farm's mill house and then the farmhouse. It is quite an imposing building and was built in the late C18 but is now converted into flats.

Munslow Stocks.

The village stocks were situated at the corner of Park Lane, Munslow until 1900 and alongside was the Old Pound where livestock were impounded.

Swan Inn, Aston, Munslow.

Swan Inn, Aston Munslow.

Aston Munslow was originally named Estune, meaning the eastern farm or enclosure. Estune became Aston but as there were several Astons it was named Munslow Aston, later to become Aston Munslow. The black and white Swan Inn was once named the Hundred House, possibly due to it being the venue for meetings of the lower Munslow divisional magistrates. It stands on the junction beside the B4368 and the lane that leads to the village. The Swan's first licence was granted in 1790 although the building is claimed to be as early as 1350 and there are claims that it is the oldest licensed premises in Shropshire. The trustees of Ludlow Municipal Charities owned the pub in 1896. In 1902 it was owned by the Ludlow and Craven Arms Brewery. A market was held from time to time in the old orchard on the opposite side of the B4368. The road was known as the Apostles Way and in 1756 it was converted to a turnpike road. The tarmac covered car park, adjacent to the Swan, was and still is the village green. There is a story that the famous highwayman Dick Turpin 1705-1739 stopped at the Swan and a sign situated at the side of the B4368 stated, *"Dick Turpin stopped here, why don't you"*.

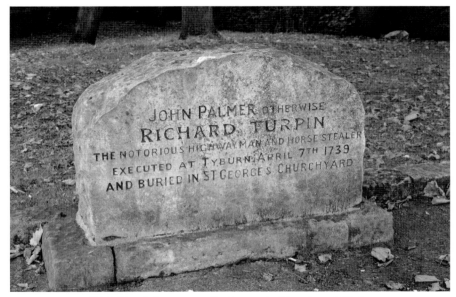

Dick Turpin's grave at St. George's Churchyard, York.

The two black and white cottages over the B4368 from the Swan Inn were owned by the Bache Mill born, entrepreneur, Freddie Freeman in 1900. His brother and sister in law lived in the western one which had nine acres attached to it. He also owned the two cottages to the east and a smallholding that later was to have Aston Munslow Garage, two houses and a bungalow built on it. Mrs Ada Austin (Mother of Eddie Austin) lived in the western cottage, which was also the village shop. Just a little further to the west, Fred erected a wooden bungalow and this property became the home of Jack Shaw who was the local policeman. Robert White bought this bungalow when Jack and his wife died in 1984 and two years later, replaced it with a new bungalow named 'Springfield'. Freddie Freeman lived nearby in 'The Cottage' and kept the blacksmith's forge there and another forge at Bouldon. 'The Cottage' was built in 1640 and in 1902 the thatched roof was replaced with tiles. An extension was added to house a doctor's surgery and police office for Sergeant Jack Shaw to enforce sheep dipping and gun licences. In 1923 William Foulkes bought the cottage. He milked cows and delivered milk to the houses using a small trailer behind a bicycle. Freddie Freeman moved to 'Rose Cottage' on the north side of the B4368. He gave up the Bouldon forge in 1912 and moved into Beambridge forge. Whilst at Beambridge, Fred had a pair of good working horses that he used to 'tush' timber out of the woods for the Millichope estate. He owned the village shop, Little Ash Cottage, the bakery and Post Office at Munslow. He also ran a coal haulage business with a, model 'T' Ford, one ton lorry. This vehicle, with a purpose built body fitted on top with seats down each side and access steps at the rear, was converted into the local bus that did regular trips to markets. Fred held the first Public Service Vehicle Operator's Licence from Ludlow to Bridgnorth which he later sold to Morgans of Wye Valley Motors, Hereford. Fred took over the route from Stanton Long to Ludlow via Bouldon and Peaton from Taffy Evans and his wife Audrey who had operated a vehicle similar in design to Fred's. It was quite amusing when Taffy would often start off without looking to see if Audrey was on board and she had to scramble up the rear steps to get on the vehicle. She was well liked and did shopping in Ludlow for folk and delivered it back to their homes from the bus.

In 1946 Frank Johnson bought the nine acres of land belonging to the cottage. He sold a field at the rear but kept the strip that he then built the Aston Munslow garage on. In the 1970s Eddie Leggit bought the garage and built a bungalow on the east side and a retail shop at the garage. Later a house was built at each end of the property. Eddie retired and Mike Lewis took over and expanded the business.

Fred Jordan 'A real Shropshire Lad' was born at Ludlow in 1922 and spent all of his working life as a farm worker, spending several years working for Burgoynes of Sparchford. They were agricultural contractors and Fred would travel south Shropshire doing general farmwork – thrashing, 'pleaching' hedges, digging ditches etc. But he was more famous for his folk singing, on BBC Radio and venues all over Great Britain. In 1958 he sang in London's Cecil Sharp House, the Spinners Folk Club in Liverpool, Royal Festival Hall London, Free Trade Hall Manchester and Royal Albert Hall London in 1971. Although he enjoyed the big venues he was never as happy as when he was singing at the Green Dragon and Hen & Chickens at Ludlow or his regular, Saturday evening, at the Buck's Head, Hungerford. Fred was a jovial character and lived for many years at Washwell Cottage near to the Swan at Aston Munslow. It was so named because the villagers used a shallow well nearby for washing only. Drinking water was in a well fifty yards distant. Both wells were used until the mains water supply arrived in the 1930s. Fred was still singing at Ripon, Fleetwood, Nottingham and London in 1998. Sadly he died in 2002 aged 80.

Aston Hall, Aston Munslow.

Probably the most important house in the parish in the C17 was the stone built, Aston Hall. It was once the home of the Baldwin family, ancestors of Earl Stanley Baldwin, 1st Earl of Bewdley, Viscount Corvedale and Conservative Prime Minister three times between 1923 and 1937. John Smith, Baron of the exchequer, owned the hall and it stayed in his family until 1911 when it was sold to P G Holder. Mainly Elizabethan, the northwest wing is the oldest part of the E shaped house. The large star shaped chimneys; fine oak panelling and oak staircase are impressive. Three servants looked after the hall in 1939 although there were many more in earlier years. The Aston estate at one time exceeded 800 acres but much of it has been sold off. 200 acres went to the Race House situated just west of the Hall. In 1912, Major J.I.Benson bought the Hall with 100 acres off P.G. Holder. The Benson family sold the Hall in 1978 with only 13 acres remaining and it is presently for sale again, with an asking price of £1.5 million.

Aston Munslow's Wesleyan Methodist Chapel.

Built of Aymestrey limestone, it was opened on 13th November, 1862 and remained open until 2006. It is now a private dwelling.

This **Wesleyan Methodist Church van** toured the area of the Corvedale from 1865 until 1914. It was used throughout the period and during the building of the various Methodist Chapels. The assistance of a local horse owner would be enlisted to move the van on to the next venue. It is believed that this photo was taken in 1910.

The White House at Aston Munslow was built for Roger Stedman in 1335 and remained in the Stedman family until 1946. The stuccoed Georgian front was added right across the southern end of the building after a fire in 1780.

The rear of the White House – showing the C16 additions. It is thought that it was once four houses, although, from the outside it, looks like one. The earliest part of the building is the long cruck hall that was built in the C14.

You can see that the **White House fireplace** is very early and was probably where the fire of 1780 started. Restoration followed the fire and included further additions and alterations - a new drawing room, staircase, hall and a main bedroom. Miss Constance Purser became the new owner and opened the house up as a museum until 1990 when the Landmark Trust took it over and are anxious to preserve the interesting buildings. To fund the project the house is let out as holiday accommodation.

Eddie Austin, aged 18 with Freeman's bus outside Ludlow Town Hall. Eddie Austin, nephew of Freddie Freeman was born in 1919 and always lived in Munslow parish. He left school to become a conductor on his uncle's bus. Eddie served in the army throughout WWII and returned to his old job in 1946, moving to the front of the bus to become driver.

Eddie Austin with his bus.

Eddie started his own one – man business in 1948 and carried schoolchildren to Culmington School for up to three generations of a family. He started the day with a newspaper round at 4.30 am, transported children to Culmington and Church Stretton schools and workers to Chukie Chickens at Craven Arms. He would organise trips to the theatres and the Granada Cinema in Shrewsbury. One of his favourite jobs was transporting football teams to their away fixtures. On his retirement at the age of 65 in 1983, he said he had been lucky in that he had never had a day off work in all his working life and would continue with his paper round while he was able. Eddie passed away in 2002.

Brown Clee from Little London.

High above and north of Aston Munslow is a settlement known as Little London. This picture was taken from Little London, looking out at the Brown Clee. Several areas throughout the country have a Little London and it usually means an area taken over by drovers or squatters. The Corvedale had several such areas, Balaam's Heath, Tugford Green in front of the church (both in Tugford Parish), Hayton's Bent and Aston Munslow.

Squatters Cottage.

From the late C16 until the late C18, the rationalisation of farm holdings and the creation of a landless, peasant class led to these people encroaching upon common wastelands as 'squatters'. They would erect crude, one room cottages and enclose a small area of land which they would then work as their own. Initially they were fined 6d a year, but after 20 years they would be put on to the manor rent roll. In 1843, Little London in Aston Munslow had 43 enclosures and several properties of which only three now remain – Starting Gate Cottage, White Lodge and Well Cottage. Little London farm is a recent construction on what was Coppice Piece, with a coppice between it and Aston Deans. In 1980 the farm bungalow and 45 acres became a National Hunt racing yard under trainer Ken White who retired and closed the stables in 1995.

BRONCROFT CASTLE

Broncroft Castle.

Originally named Bromcroft in 1086 because of the broom covered area that contained a croft or dwelling, belonging to Corfham castle. Broncroft Castle was built on a former Saxon and Norman site in about 1382 by the Burley family who came from Burley in Herefordshire. They were not aristocracy, but wealthy civil servants, who were close to King Richard II. Despite this, one member of the family, Sir Simon Burley, was beheaded in the first execution at Tower Hill in 1388 (supposedly against the King's wishes). In 1470, the castle passed to the Littleton family through marriage and they retained it until the mid C16, when the Lutley family from Enville in Staffordshire, exchanged their (old school) home in Munslow with the Littletons of Broncroft Castle. The Littletons retained the Broncroft deer park. The park consisted of Broncroft Lodge, Broncroft Park and Upper Park, now known as Earnstrey. In 1334, Hugh Tyrell the tenant of the park and his heirs forever, were granted the right to rear rabbits which were first imported by the Normans. The castle was garrisoned by Adam Lutley for the King in 1642 but he later damaged it, leaving it abandoned and unusable. Lord Calvin's Parliamentarian forces re-occupied the castle in 1645. Three hundred and fifty Royalists fought a fierce skirmish outside the castle, capturing fifty two Parliamentarian prisoners and eighty horses but did not take the castle. In 1648 the castle was thought to be of no purpose and they left it merely as a farmhouse for two centuries. In 1807 the last of the Lutley descendants sold the castle remains. It changed hands several times before it was restored to a habitable castle about 1872 by the owners since 1817, the Johnstone family, who were originally from Ludlow.

Broncroft Castle Meet.

In 1889, the Whitaker family extended and improved the castle. This postcard of 1909 shows Henry Whittaker at his Broncroft Castle home with the meet of the hounds. Only the tower to the right of the entrance is original, the rest being Victorian. It is now a Grade II listed private residence. Sir Thomas Littleton sold Broncroft deer park to John Walcot of Walcot in 1657; Hugh Walcot sold it to Andrew Hill of Henley Hall in 1737 for £3,150. In 1752 it was sold to the descendants of the Lutley family – thus reuniting the park and castle.

Broncroft Lower Parks is a C17 timber framed farmhouse, tenanted by several farmers throughout two centuries. Arthur Stedman farmed here until his death in 1669. The church commissioners bought the property with land from Mr Whitaker in 1922. The Beazley family farmed here from 1942 and later purchased the farm from the church commissioners. It is still farmed by the Beazley family.

Broncroft Lodge Farm.

The largest of the Broncroft farms is the C18 brick built Lodge Farm that had replaced an earlier C16 hunting lodge where Mr John Barbor resided in 1580. The farm was over 300 acres in size and much of it adjoined the river Corve. It was tenanted by the Turner family throughout much of the C18 and C19 until it was purchased by the Evans family who farmed there from 1881 until 1989. They were followed by the Hughes family. The site of the lost medieval village of Marston is situated nearby. Broncroft mill was situated on Lodge Farm and the present building goes back to the mid C18 although an earlier mill probably stood on this site. William Yapp was miller in 1851 but from then until 1881 the mill ceased working. John Davis was miller here from 1881 until 1913 when Edwin Welson took over and he was the last miller at Broncroft mill, finishing in the mid 1920's. The mill became the laundry for Broncroft Castle and later was converted to a private house.

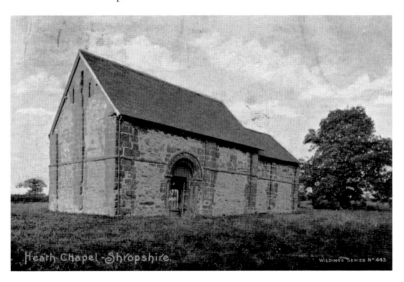

Heath Chapel.

A C12 chapel (of no known dedication) is situated 790 feet above sea level, at the Heath (a township of Stoke St Milborough parish), in the middle of a field, adjoining a medieval village of some four hectares. It is a typical example of a compact Norman church, without a bell tower and without any decoration besides chevron mouldings on the doorway. The interior is basic but quaint with a cylindrical tub font. A Communion rail, pulpit, reader's desk and pews were installed in the C17. Services were held monthly in 1719, twice monthly in the late C20 and four families attended regularly in 1965. The nave roof was renewed in the C17, the stone work restored in the C19 and it is now a Grade I listed building which is well worth a visit.

The Chapel has had several famous visitors over the years. Princess Mary, later to become Queen Mary, paid a visit in 1926 and also the Archbishop of York. In 1927 Stanley Baldwin, whose descendants were from the Corvedale, entered his name in the Chapel's visitors' book. Stanley, born in 1867, was a formidable character and was the son of Alfred Baldwin, the head of the Baldwin's of Bewdley which was one of the largest iron and steel works in Britain in its time. Stanley went into politics as a Conservative member of parliament and became Prime Minister three times between the two wars. He was the only Prime Minister to serve under three Monarchs - Kings, George V, Edward VIII and George VI. In 1919 he donated a fifth of his wealth (approx £3,000,000 in today's money) to help reduce the war debt. His titles were Viscount Corvedale and Earl Baldwin of Bewdley. He died in 1947 aged 80. In 1815 the original five Heath farms were merged into two, Upper Heath Farm and Heath House Farm.

Bouldon Village.

Bouldon started out in 1086 as "Bolledone", the name probably derived from the Saxon, meaning 'a settlement on a hill'. Bouldon is 476ft above sea level at the eastern boundary of the Corvedale and on the edge of the Clee Hills, one mile south of Broncroft Castle. It is a C16 and C17 stone built village in the shape of a triangle and it had eight houses in 1672. Four timber cottages for farm workers' were erected by the Church Commissioners in the 1950s.

Bouldon Village.

Little has changed since the 1950s. Sheep and cattle have been raised in the Corvedale for centuries and that continues today. The average size of a Corvedale farm is 280 acres. A fair amount of arable farming has played a big part in the fertile valley with the growing of corn and animal fodder. Only three dairy farms are left in the Corvedale at present. It was once a very industrious village based around the turnpike road between Ludlow and Bridgnorth from 1794 until 1873. Bouldon was bypassed in 1879 when the road was re-routed to the east of Brown Clee Hill.

Tally Ho Inn, Bouldon.

Bouldon boasts a village inn named the 'Tally Ho', opened in 1844, to allow travellers to quench their thirst. Later, the village shop was opened at the front of the pub and was kept by Thomas and Susannah Francis when Caddick took this photo. Tragedy struck the Francis family at the Tally Ho in 1916 when they received a telegram to say their son William had been killed. The next day they received another telegram to say their other son Thomas had been killed.

FRANCIS, Private, William Orlando, 18036. Born Montgomery. 7th Bn. King's Shropshire Light Infantry. Died of wounds 2nd April 1916. Age 25. Son of Thomas and Susannah Francis, buried at Burn Lijssenthoek Military Cemetery, Poperinge.

FRANCIS, Private, Thomas, 18035. Born Montgomery. 7th Bn. King's Shropshire Light Infantry. Killed in action 3rd April 1916. Age 23. Son of Thomas and Susannah Francis. His name is on the Menin Gate. The Tally Ho closed in 2006 and reopened again in 2012. It is now renowned as a place to visit for a good meal and a pint of real ale.

Tally Ho, Bouldon.

The picture shows Sidney Caddick, the photographer, using one of his many skills in giving a display of Punch and Judy for the villagers outside the Tally Ho.

The Lock family Fiddlers played their fiddles in several Corvedale pubs and throughout South Shropshire, including The Tally Ho.

Bouldon Mill.

One of the industries in Bouldon was the corn mill which was originally built of timber in 1611. It was rebuilt in stone in 1790 and from 1803 until 1850 was producing paper. This postcard shows residents, Mr and Mrs Edward Page, who were there from 1896 until 1915.

Bouldon Mill was driven by water from the Pye Brook at the east of the village. It drove a Coalbrookdale cast iron water wheel that is still in situ today. The mill ceased working in 1934, leaving it as a private residence which is for sale now for £599,950. Bouldon had a charcoal fuelled ironworks of its own producing pig iron, tenanted by the Blount family in C17 and C18. In 1644, iron, to make a gun for the defence of Ludlow, was supplied. Four hundred tons of the finest quality pig iron was produced and transported from Bouldon in 1717. It closed around 1795 and only a tree covered slag heap remains.

The road mending gang who would use the Bouldon stone to repair the Corvedale Road. Notice the lorry with two men sat on the back and the horse drawn tar melter on metal wheels. Seymour Stephens, from Bushmoor, is fifth from right.

Bouldon Chapel.

A Chapel of ease is believed to have been located at Bouldon Farm in the C18, where burials have been found. In 1873 the corrugated iron chapel of "All Saints" was erected at the expense of the rector of Holdgate. In 1900 they held a weekly service and it continued in use until 1981 when it was sold for £5,000 and later demolished. A house was built on the site.

Now on to Diddlebury.

Diddlebury is derived from 'Duddela's Burgh' or the manor of a Saxon named Duddela. The Diddle brook rises at Wetmore, runs through Middlehope and enters the Corvedale just before Bache Mill before going through Diddlebury and entering the river Corve between Lawton and Sparchford.

Diddlebury Church.

One of the oldest churches in Shropshire is St Peter's Church at Diddlebury, probably dating back to 1010. On the north side interior of the nave is pre- conquest herringbone walling. The C12 saw the church extended substantially and a south aisle was added in the C13. A porch was erected in 1884. The Saxon tower has been rebuilt several times which is indicated by the various wide buttresses surrounding the base. It houses four bells and a clock. There are five stained glass windows with the east window representing the Crucifixion. In 1900 the bell frame was renewed, the bells re-hung at a cost of £112 and the tower was again restored at a cost of £1,300.

The Lych Gate – Diddlebury.

WILDING Nº 1581.

Diddlebury Lych Gate, School and Church.

Adjacent to the church is the old school, built on the site of an earlier grammar school where Lord Herbert of Chirbury was educated between 1592 and 1594. The school (as seen in the picture between the church and the lych gate) was built in 1789 at a cost of £34.12s.3d and rebuilt in 1834 at a cost of £28.10s. The lych gate was dedicated in October 1908 – two years before the photo was taken. The house shown on the left of the church is the Church Farmhouse where Sidney Corfield and his son Brian lived in later years.

Diddlebury School.

was built in the village to seat 150 pupils. Here we see the schoolchildren outside the school house with headmaster John Rowland Jones on the right of the picture and his wife Henrietta, left of the doorway, in 1905. John was headmaster from 1892 until 1909. Sadly, he died in the same year as his retirement after falling from his bicycle. His wife Henrietta continued teaching at the school until 1924 when she was sixty years old. In the 1980's Munslow, Culmington and Stanton Lacy schools all combined into Diddlebury School. In 1998, farmer Michael Wilkes gave the school half an acre to increase the recreational area. The old school became the clubroom and reading room of the Working Men's Club. The Millennium then saw its conversion into a community room.

A young Brian Corfield (from Church Farm, Diddlebury) taking his father's horse into a hayfield where he turned and dried the hay ready for baling.

Diddlebury Youth Club.

1970 Saw the youth club meeting at the old school room next to the church. At the back are the three youth club leaders – Win Price, John Pearce and Bob Humphreys.

Diddlebury Corner.

Caddick has captioned his postcard 'Delbury' rather than Diddlebury – the locally used derivation of the name.

Rosemary Leach.

This pretty little girl caught the eye of Caddick and he could not resist taking her picture. She was Rosemary Leach and she was born on 18th December 1935 – the daughter of the then headmaster at Diddlebury school. She attended RADA and went on to appear in repertory theatres and at the Old Vic. She was regularly on TV in such as The Power Game, The Jewel in the Crown, Day to Remember and The Charmer opposite Nigel Havers. She was nominated six times for a Bafta Award and won the Olivier Award in 1982 for the best actress in a new play – "84 Charing Cross Road". More recently she appeared in "Margaret" in 2009.

Old Thatched Cottage at Bach Mill, Diddlebury, Shropshire.

Bach Mill.

This scene has changed very little in the hundred years that has passed since Wilding took this picture of Bach Mill, Diddlebury, except that the thatched roofs are now slated. Before being 'swallowed' up by neighbouring Diddlebury, this was the more important settlement of the two. In 1841, the sole landowner was Herbert Cornewall. James Dyer was the local carpenter, Samuel Hancocks the blacksmith, Joseph Sankey was tailor and shopkeeper, Richard Sankey was a tailor and the postmaster. John Stubbs was a shopkeeper, John Owen a shoemaker and John Clinton the wheelwright. The actual mill was named Rookes Mill up until the 1950s after Frances Rooke who was the miller in 1890.

Glebe Farm.

In the C11 the eight clergy of Diddlebury lived at a large hall situated where Glebe Farm now stands. It was in very poor condition by 1458 and the one remaining vicar moved to the rectory at Corfton. The old hall with its farmland was then leased out to William Baldwyn, and it remained with numerous leaseholders until 1913 when Edwin Cox, late of the Sun Inn Corfton, purchased it. The Wilkes family purchased it in 1952.

DIDDLEBURY - GLEBE FARM - HEREFORD STOCK BULL.

Jackson on bull.

The owner of Glebe farm, Edwin Cox, was well known as a breeder of Hackney horses as well as a Hereford cattle breeder. He was also clerk to the parish council. Here is his worker 'Jackson' on board a fine example of a Hereford bull at Glebe Farm in 1914.

Diddlebury Vicarage-Shropshire.

Diddlebury Vicarage.

In 1884, a new vicarage was built in Diddlebury and the vicar of the time, Rev Andrew Pope moved in. The three storey vicarage contained ten bedrooms and four reception rooms. It was built in natural stone with interesting, brick contrast detail and timbered gables. The attractive open porch has mosaic flooring and stained glass detail to the main entrance. 56 acres of glebe farmland surrounded the vicarage which had a range of farm buildings. It is presently for sale at £850,000 with two acres of land.

Rev Goodwin Purcell and Mrs Purcell outside Diddlebury Vicarage in 1923, ready to visit some parishioners in their smart transport of the day. The very large parish of Diddlebury consisted, in those days, of twelve hamlets; Westhope, Great Sutton, Little Sutton, Lawton, Peaton, Broncroft, Middlehope, Corfton, Sparchford, Earnstrey Park, Abdon and Bouldon.

Delbury Hall.

This early 1906 Wilding postcard shows clearly, the wings added in 1836. Delbury Hall has been standing in one form or another since the C14 when John Baldwyn was living there. The title 'Delbury Hall' is just a grander version of Diddlebury Hall. The Baldwyn family remained there until 1752 when it was sold to the Cornewall family of Burford for £9,854. Frederick Cornewall almost totally rebuilt the house, leaving only part of the old house and malthouse at the rear of the new red bricked house that had cost £1,757 including the interior decorations. By 1827, two pools and a park surrounded the Hall, but the one pool and the park had disappeared by 1883. In 1845 the Cornewall family rented out the hall until it was sold to Captain Wingfield Stratford in 1910.

Delbury Hall.

The front porch had been added to the hall and it looked a more homely, mature home when Caddick took this picture in 1941.

The dovecote at Delbury Hall provided meat for the residents.

Vincent Shires Wrigley.

Captain Wingfield Stratford then sold the hall to Vincent Shires Wrigley in 1922. Vincent is seen here in the grounds of Delbury Hall. He had been a Lancashire cotton manufacturer before he moved to Eriviat Hall in Denbighshire and then to Delbury Hall. During WWII, ammunition was stored in the grounds of the hall and a small railway ran between the ammunition Nissan huts. His grandson Patrick Wrigley is still in residence at the hall but sold much of the estate off in the 1990s.

Diddlebury Tenant Farmers.

This is a photo of the tenant farmers on the Delbury estate, meeting at Delbury Hall in 1965 and celebrating the marriage of Miss Rosamaund Wrigley to Mr C Woodward.

Back Row: Harry Jarvis, keeper, Price Brown, Charles Pugh, Elsie Woodhouse, Stan Carter, Arthur Woodhouse, Greta Yapp, David Yapp.

Middle Row: Joe Kilvert, Graham Coles, Mrs Pugh, Kathleen Woodhouse, Bill Woodhouse.

Front Row: Renee Morris, Mrs Kilvert, Hilda Carter, George Morris, Amy Morris, Dorothy Kilvert, Eddie Morris.

Delbury Farm has a long history, with the acreage changing from 700 acres in 1851 to 300 acres in 1871 and 720 acres in 1891, all under the landlords of the Delbury Estate. In 1910 the Delbury Estate was sold to P.G. Holder who then sold 173 acres with Delbury Farm to the tenant Morgan Jones, who became the first Diddlebury owner occupier. P.G. Holder added the remainder of the farm to his own estate. Glendower Jones farmed there after WW1 until 1931 when he moved to Stokesay Castle Farm. Charles Pryce bought Delbury farm and remained there until 1950. John Morgan became the owner until his death in 1994. The farmhouse was sold but the land is still farmed by John Morgan's son from a new farmhouse. The Caddick glass plate tells us that it was Pryce's farm when the photo was taken in 1937.

Harvesting at Hale Farm.

In 1932 Miss Dorothy Kilvert and her brother Joe moved into Hale Farm, (between Diddlebury and Corfton) on the north side of the B4368. Dorothy was a keen horse woman and an accomplished rider. She kept thoroughbreds and hunters and won numerous awards. Joe is seen here on his Fordson Standard tractor towing a binder. Dorothy retired in 1998 and later died at Hale Farm.

Diddlebury Post Office.

John Stubbs was sub postmaster in Diddlebury before unmarried sisters Sara, Martha and Marianne Sankey added the Post Office to their dressmaking and grocers shop on the B4368 road. Sara kept the shop for nearly fifty years, until her death about 1909. She was followed by Charles Edwards and then William Jones. The post office was later closed and moved to Aston Munslow.

Snow cutting at Pinstones lane in 1947, one of the worst winters in living memory. Many farms were cut off for several weeks that year. The Pinstones farm was built on the old common and was originally named Hale Head and later Pinson's before becoming Pinstones. Common land in several locations of the Corvedale grew whimberries which locals would pick to make whimberry and apple pie. In good years they were picked and taken to wholesalers who would send them to Lancashire where they were used for dye in the textile industry. The decline in common land meant the decline in whimberries and also the decline of bullfinches, chaffinches and goldfinches that fed on the berries.

Corfham Castle Remains.

A mile E.S.E. of Diddlebury, on the Peaton road, stood double- moated Corfham Castle. The moat was filled from the nearby Pye Brook. The C13 stone castle was quite a grand building and it was once one of the largest stone fortifications in Shropshire. By 1550 only one tower remained standing. In 1177, Walter de Clifford was granted Corfham for services rendered. Walter was the father of Fair Rosamund 1136-1176, who was King Henry II's mistress. Corfham had a chapel up until C15 which suggests that there was originally a Corfham settlement. If there had been an early Corfham settlement it may have been wiped out by the 1348 Black Death plague.

Richard Shirley and his family at C17 Baucott Farm.

Fertecote was the original name of Baucott, changing to Balcot after Roger de Balcot and finishing up as Baucott. It had eight tenant farmers in 1770 but only three are there today. John Sheppard farmed here in 1553 and his descendant Francis Sheppard, killed Richard More, son of Jasper More in a duel in 1608. Francis emigrated to avoid conflict and joined the army in Ireland. He amassed a fortune in land taken from the rebels. The Shirley family farmed at Baucott from 1834 and Richard Shirley was a celebrated breeder of Hereford cattle. He exported bulls to America and New Zealand in 1884.

The Hereford bull is one of the UK's oldest native beef breeds, originating in the county of Herefordshire in the mid 1700's and later spreading to most parts of the UK and the rest of the world. The Hereford Cattle Society was founded under the patronage of Queen Victoria in 1878. The Herd Book was opened in 1846 and since 1886 has been closed to any animal whose sire or dam had not previously been recorded. So for over 120 years, the purity of the breed has remained intact.

Baucott Farm.

You may wonder why the 'Stars and Stripes' American flag is flying in this picture of Baucott Farm in 1977. It was put there by Stephen Williams of Baucott to welcome descendants of an American cattle buyer who was visiting to see where his ancestor's Hereford cattle had been bred in 1884 by Mr Richard Shirley. Baucott had a chapel until 1138 when it was amalgamated with Tugford chapel. The John Family farmed both Baucott Farm and Baucott Manor farm from the 1920s. Stephen Williams took over Baucott Farm in 1952 and stayed until his retirement. The Teague family now farm both holdings.

This is the modernised 'Poor House of Balaam's Heath'.

A poor house, or Victorian workhouse, was supported at the expense of the public and was where those who had fallen on hard times were housed. They were usually local people who were poor, elderly and often disabled and they would have to work at the nearby farms to earn their keep. The Social Security Act came into force in 1935 and the need for a Poor House declined and by 1950 they had almost completely disappeared.

Balaam's Heath, north of Baucott was 300 acres of boggy common ground used by tenants of the Tugford Manor. In 1680 there were just two cottages and by 1851 there were eighteen but they declined to four in 1989. In 1815 the remaining common of ninety one acres was enclosed. A Balaam's Heath society of Primitive Methodists held meetings in 1832 and Mary Sargeon 'A wise woman' died at the age of 104 in the same year. William Dodson was a wheelwright at Balaam's Heath in 1881.

Peaton Strand Primitive Methodist Chapel opened in 1873 and closed in 1985, it was demolished, leaving only the decorative bricks in the lower wall. This photo shows the congregation emerging after the last harvest festival service at the Methodist Chapel at Peaton Strand, held in September 1984.

The Methodist Chapel house at Peaton Strand was left standing when the Chapel was demolished, leaving only the decorative bricks in the lower wall of the chapel showing. Peaton Strand is a hamlet of a few cottages between Bouldon and Peaton which is partly situated in the valley of the Strand Brook and partly along the lane to Bouldon where the Strand Brook has its confluence with the larger Pye Brook. In the 1950s, four timber cottages were built in the Strand for farm workers by the Church Commissioners.

Peaton Hall.

A date in stone tells us that Peaton Hall was built in 1663 and another dated stone gives 1920 as the date that the Hall was refurbished. The Hall was a gentleman farmer's residence owned by the Earls of Stafford and rented out to the Pulley family in the C17. Emblems of the Earls of Shrewsbury and the Earls of Stafford, The Talbot and the Staffordshire Knot, are carved in the stone of a nearby Hall building commemorating that the two families once owned the property. The Hall had up to 900 acres of farmland attached, but acreage varied when parts were rented out to other neighbouring farms by the landlords. In 1897, a Ludlow banker, W.H. Atherden bought the Hall and transformed the front of it by adding bay windows and a porch.

P.G. Holder bought Peaton Hall in 1930 and created a gigantic dairy herd with a cow house that was reputed to be the largest in Europe, with 288 cows under one roof.

EUROPE'S LARGEST COWHOUSE

Farmer and Stock-Breeder Photograph

AT PEATON HALL, CRAVEN ARMS. FOR P. G. HOLDER, ESQ.
STRUCTURAL FRAMEWORK, ROOFING, GLAZING, WINDOWS, ETC., BY W. H. SMITH & CO. (WHITCHURCH) LTD.

Reputedly the largest cowhouse in Europe was built by W.H.Smith of Whitchurch and housed the very latest dairy equipment. A railway was built to transport the ten gallon churns to the main road where it was collected by lorry and delivered to Cadbury's at Marlbrook, Leominster. Unfortunately the whole herd was later wiped out by brucellosis. A piggery was established on the farm but that also was wiped out by swine fever. During the 1939 winter over a thousand sheep were frozen to death on the Hall Farm. P.G.Holder moved out and the empty cow house found a new life when it was occupied by Hurry Heaters from Birmingham. They made fuel tanks for Stirling bombers from 1940 until 1944 and employed men and women from the Corvedale, Ludlow and Birmingham areas. A security office still stands to this day. Electricity was made available for the factory but the Corvedale had to wait until after the war. Peaton Hall was converted into offices for the factory. After the war Mr John Thomas took over the tenancy and his son Mervyn still farms there today.

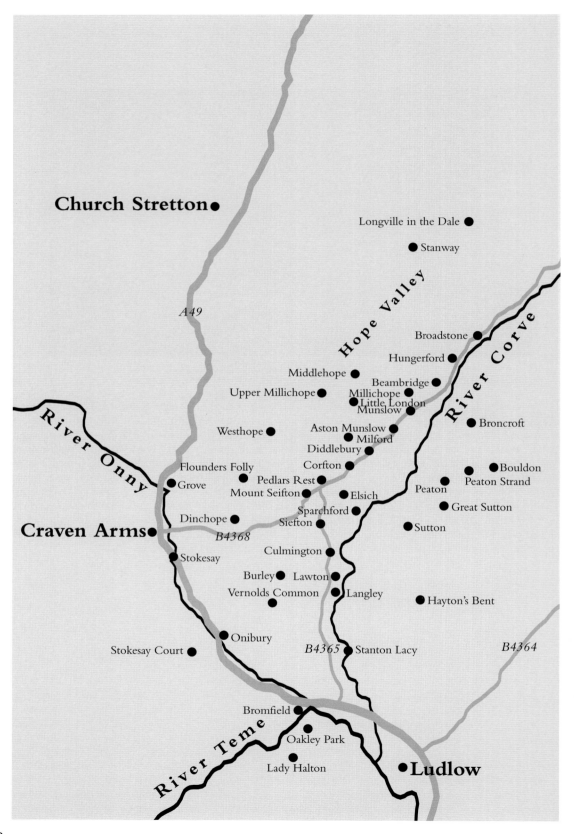

Church Stretton●

Longville in the Dale ●

● Stanway

Hope Valley

River Corve

A49

Broadstone ●

Hungerford ●

Middlehope ●

Beambridge ●
Upper Millichope ●   Millichope ●
Little London ●
Munslow ●

Broncroft ●

Westhope ●   Aston Munslow ●
Milford ●
Diddlebury ●

River Onny

Flounders Folly   Corfton ●
● Grove   ● Pedlars Rest ●
Mount Seifton ●   Elsich ●
Dinchope ●   Sparchford ●
Craven Arms●   Siefton ●

Bouldon ●
Peaton Strand
Peaton ●
Great Sutton ●

B4368

Culmington ●

Sutton ●

Stokesay ●

Burley ●   Lawton ●
Vernolds Common ●   Langley ●

Hayton's Bent ●

Onibury ●

B4365   Stanton Lacy ●

B4364

Stokesay Court ●

Bromfield ●

River Teme

Oakley Park ●

Lady Halton ●

●Ludlow

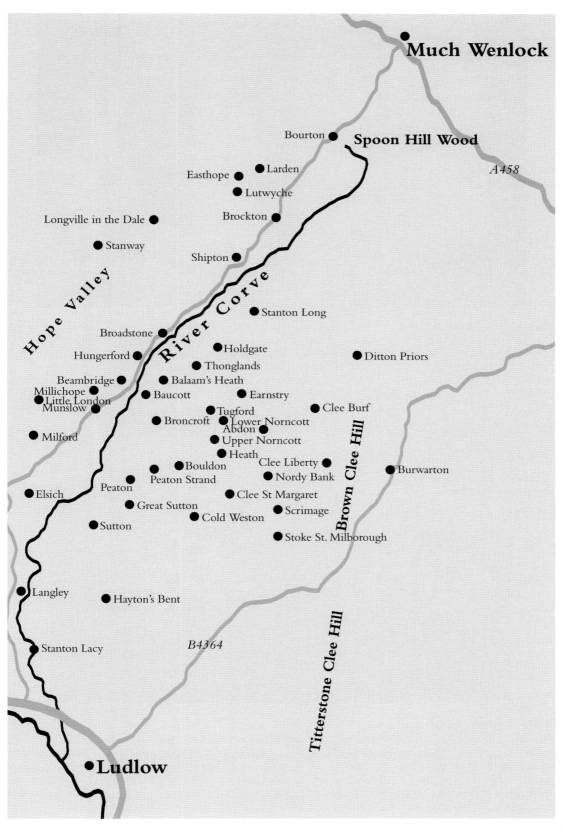

Much Wenlock

Bourton **Spoon Hill Wood**

A458

Larden

Easthope

Lutwyche

Longville in the Dale

Brockton

Stanway

Shipton

Hope Valley

River Corve

Stanton Long

Broadstone

Holdgate

Ditton Priors

Hungerford

Thonglands

Beambridge

Balaam's Heath

Millichope

Baucott

Earnstry

Little London

Clee Burf

Munslow

Tugford

Broncroft

Lower Norncott

Abdon

Milford

Upper Norncott

Heath

Clee Liberty

Brown Clee Hill

Bouldon

Burwarton

Peaton Strand

Nordy Bank

Peaton

Elsich

Clee St Margaret

Great Sutton

Scrimage

Cold Weston

Sutton

Stoke St. Milborough

Langley

Hayton's Bent

Stanton Lacy

B4364

Titterstone Clee Hill

Ludlow

Westhope Manor Staff.
Katie Peacock, Fred Wallace, ---?, Charlie Neil, ---?, Joe Carter and daughter, Cissie Carter.
Fred Wallace became chauffer at Westhope Manor after leaving the Royal Air Force in 1919.

Ward Farm, Westhope.
There was a Ward Farm at Westhope in 1602 and it could have been built even before that. Colonel Swinnerton Dyer demolished the ancient Ward House and used much of the oak to build the new Ward Farmhouse late in 1891. The farm is presently an organic working farm and has a B&B business at the house.

Peaton Lodge.

Nearby Peaton Lodge is a C17, stone built house, probably the original farmhouse to Peaton Hall. It has a central stair passage which gives it an air of opulence, endorsing the fact that it was once more than a farmhouse. The land belonging to the lodge over the years ranged from 350 acres down to 90 acres and when it was sold by the Church Commissioners in 1960 there was no farmland attached. Robert and Julia Gratton bought the lodge in 1988. Opposite the Lodge are six timber cottages erected by the Church Commissioners in the 1950s

Westhope Manor.

The Manor of Westhope was held by Roger de Montgomery at the time of the Doomsday Book and it was rented to Picot de Say. The name Westhope derives from 'Hope' which in Celtic means 'valley' and, as it is to the west of Hope Valley, it has become Westhope. It is believed that a castle with a moat stood at Westhope in the early days but all that now remains is the aptly named Moat Meadow. The estate, once part of the Long Forest, was over 1,500 acres with several farms and ten cottages, owned by the Earl of Arundel in the C13 until 1561 when it was sold to Queen Elizabeth I. The Dannatt family were at Westhope during the C16 and first half of the C17 when Thomas Dannatt sold the Westhope estate in

1655. Henry Fleming from Sibdon Castle became Lord of Westhope, followed by his descendant Gilbert Fleming who died in 1774. His daughter Frances Fleming became Lady of the Manor and she died in 1792. Being the last of the Flemings to possess Westhope, She left the estate, including a £4,000 mortgage, to Sir John Swinnerton Dyer, 6th Baronet, 1738 -1801. Sir John was a wealthy man and a great friend of the then Prince of Wales, who once loaned the Prince £80,000, which was never repaid. Sir John's son, Sir Thomas Richard Swinnerton Dyer, 7th Baronet 1768-1838, took over the estate. Sir Thomas married Elizabeth Standerwicke of Ovington House, Arlesford, Hants. Sir Thomas died in 1838 and Lady Elizabeth became Lady of the Manor. She remarried in 1839 to Frederic, Baron von Zandt, chamberlain to the King of Bavaria. Frederic died in 1841 and his wife Elizabeth in 1864. The Westhope estate then went to Elizabeth's first husband's cousin, Colonel Henry Clement Swinnerton Dyer, second son of the 9th baronet, Sir Thomas Swinnerton Dyer. Henry was a military man, an ammunitions expert and later became a director in industry at Armstrong Whitworth in Newcastle. He was a well liked man and was sadly missed by all the Westhope residents when he died suddenly in 1898. His widow Emelia Susan Swinnerton Dyer became Lady of the Manor and built the new manor house. She died in 1903, leaving her son, Leonard Whitworth Swinnerton Dyer 14th Baronet 1875- 1947 as Lord of the Manor. Leonard married Lucy Schroeder of New York in 1897 and their son, Leonard Schroeder Swinnerton Dyer, 15th Baronet was born in 1898. He married Barbara Brackenbury from Seaton Burn House in Northumberland 1925.

Sir Leonard Schroeder Swinnerton Dyer
and Barbara Brackenbury's Wedding Day.

Leonard was a leading member of Shropshire County Council for many years. Lady Barbara was a keen WI member and was National President for several years. She represented the area on the council and was a stalwart in Corvedale affairs. Sir Leonard and Lady Barbara had two children - Sir Henry Peter Francis Swinnerton Dyer 16th Baronet in 1927 and Anne Winifred Swinnerton Dyer in 1932. Sir Henry now lives at Thriplow in Cambridgeshire and has had a distinguished career in mathematics, was awarded the KBE in 1987 and in 2005 he was awarded the Sylvester Medal. Anne Dyer still lives at Westhope and opened Westhope Craft College in the Dower House in 1981 with fellow co-founder Elizabeth Rumble. It provides a variety of creative craft courses. Anne also opened the Westhope Church Meadow in 1997, a one and a half acre ancient orchard Burial Ground where natural green burials are arranged. It was West Midlands Regional winner in the Peoples Award for the Best Natural Burial Ground in the UK 2013. Ann set up the Westhope Charity that now runs the College, she writes books on craftwork and in her spare time, runs the Westhope farm - a very busy and well respected lady. In 2006 she was awarded the MBE for her services to educational craft.

Ward Cottage, Westhope is a perfect example of the picturesque Westhope Manor B&W cottages on the Westhope estate. Caddick was spoilt for choice and took many photos in this area. The Cottage was built in 1906 by Mrs Martin, a sister to Sir Leonard Swinnerton Dyer and was used as a residence for the teachers at Westhope School.

Westhope Manor.

Mrs Evelyn Henrietta Martin /nee Swinnerton Dyer was a well respected lady who had married a Colonel Martin but left him soon after the honeymoon. He returned to India and Evelyn devoted herself to Westhope. She was a strong willed lady. In the 1920s she once demanded the council build a road from the White Bridge to the turn before the manor, and they did. It was for her new car, as seen here and it was the first motor car in South Shropshire.

Westhope Schoolchildren.

This photo is off a poor glass negative. These children are the pupils of Westhope School. The 60 seated black and white school was built in 1906 and was opened by the Archdeacon of Ludlow on April 8th 1907. Mrs Martin had purchased the ground off the Westhope estate. The boys at each end of the picture are both of the Manley family.

Flounders Folly, Westhope.

Benjamin Flounders.

Flounders Folly as seen by Sid Caddick in 1938.

This stone folly was built in 1838, 1085 ft above sea level, on Callow Hill, dividing four estates. It was 80ft high and 16ft square, with walls 2ft thick. It was built by a Quaker, Benjamin Flounders, supposedly to see ships docking in Liverpool. More likely it was built to give work for the locals. Benjamin had inherited the Culmington Estate in 1807, along with £200,000 from his uncle, Gideon Bickerdike, supposedly to celebrate his 70th birthday. Benjamin was born on June

17th 1768 at Yarm in Yorkshire. His father was a wealthy, bleach field owner who also had shops in Darlington; whilst his mother was a Bickerdike of Leyburn. Benjamin became an influential industrialist who had interests in timber for building ships and two linen mills. He was a director of the Stockton & Darlington Railway and owned several estates in the north. He married in 1800 and a daughter was born. His wife died and he married again but she also died in 1814. In 1817 Benjamin was baptised into the Church of England – perhaps his drinking of port and his affinity to field sports had something to do with his decision. His daughter married Major Arthur Lowe of Court Hill near Ludlow in 1841 but she died in 1844, leaving Benjamin without an heir. After losing two wives and a daughter, he was left alone and moved back to his hometown of Yarm in Yorkshire, selling Culmington Estate for £40,000 in 1845. He died the next year, aged 78.

Flounders Folly on Callow Hill, taken from the Westhope road.

Sid Caddick's photo certainly shows the Folly's splendorous position. The folly became dilapidated in the 1920s and by the 1980s it had become dangerous and in need of major restoration. Julie Christie, the well known actress, owned it for a while and in 1999 Sula Rayska, a consultant at Rayska Heritage of Shrewsbury, headed a band of like-minded people and formed the Flounders Folly Trust. They bought the folly for £1 and raised grants to fund the project. Restoration began in 2001 and, on October 31st 2005, Princess Anne performed the grand opening of the grade two listed Folly. It is now open to the public, one day a month so that people can climb to the viewing platform at the top of the 78 stairs and enjoy the wonderful views of the Longmynd hills, the Clee Hills, the Malverns, the Black Mountains, Cader Idris and the local countryside. Specially-commissioned illustrations around the viewing platform enable visitors to work out exactly what landmarks they are looking at in the landscape. A flag flies at the top on the days of opening.

Westhope Hall.

Built in 1617 and probably replacing an earlier building. It is a stone house with a brick skin. In 1925 the Prince family farmed from here and stayed until after WWII but it has since been converted into two cottages.

Middle Westhope Farm.

The Manley family have farmed at Middle Westhope, (aptly named by being the largest farm at the centre of Westhope estate), since Thomas Manley took the tenancy in 1896. Descendant Mr John Manley still farms here.

Westhope chapel dates back to at least 1255. It underwent a major restoration in 1728 by Richard Fleming, using money left by his mother in her will to rebuild the chapel. It was restored again by Colonel Swinnerton Dyer in 1892. It stands high up in an orchard where it can be seen by most of the Westhope estate. It has 11' deep stone foundations below the ground, indicating that there has been a previous chapel on the site. The foundations stand 3' above ground level and continue with red brick walls with red tiled roof. There is no graveyard. It has always been privately owned by the Lord of the Manor of Westhope. There is a seventeen inch diameter bell hung on the west gable with an inscription W. Blews & Sons 1872.

Westhope Chapel interior has several stained glass windows dedicated to the Swinnerton Dyer family. It also has a Saxon font and some carved oak furniture. An organ was presented in 1898 to replace a small harmonium and heated water pipes were installed in 1903, replacing an old stove. The chapel is still used for occasional services.

Hill End Farm, Westhope.

Another C17 farmhouse on the estate was Hill End. Thirty one year old Charles Yapp took the tenancy in 1871, leaving his former job as Waggoner on his father's farm at Middlehope. Edward Jones was the new tenant in 1900 and in 1911 the Corfield family took it over until after WWII and were then followed by the Hall family. The ground was later separated from the farmhouse.

One cannot write about Westhope without mentioning the undulating countryside that is brimming with rural serenity. This part of the Hope Valley is sheltered and rich in beauty, especially when the evening sun gleams across the upland slopes.

Lower Dinchope is at the western most tip of the Hope Valley and is just a stone's throw from Craven Arms. It is deviating slightly from the Corvedale, but with the author's love of horses it could not be left out. In 1921, Mr Tom Jones Evans, a keen Welsh Cob enthusiast, moved from Cardiganshire to Lower Dinchope Farm. He was a tenant of Harriet Rowland Greene, owner of the Grove estate at Craven Arms. She had founded the Grove Stud of Welsh Mountain ponies in 1906. Tom Jones Evans became a close friend of Harriet's and used to show her ponies at the various shows. They exported many ponies to America and at one time kept over one hundred. In 1927 Harriet was nearing seventy years of age and decided to sell most of her remaining stud of over forty ponies.

**Grove Sprightly winning at the Royal Welsh Show,
Postcard by P B Abery, Builth Wells.**

Lady Wentworth and Tom Jones Evans jointly bought a beautiful pony named Grove Sprightly at the Grove sale for 126 guineas. Three years later Tom bought Lady Wentworth's share and owned the pony outright. Grove Sprightly then went on to become champion seven times in succession at the Royal Welsh Show, a feat never to be equalled.

Dinchope Barn Gravestones.

When Grove Sprightly died in 1949, at the age of thirty-one, he had won more prizes than any other pony of his breed. He was buried at Dinchope barn and a gravestone was erected that stands to this day. The barn is still named Grove Sprightly Barn. The horse shoe gravestone alongside is to Grove Sprightly's grandfather, Bleddfa Shooting Star.

Bleddfa Shooting Star.

Another great stallion. He had been buried at the Grove and, when Harriet Greene died and the estate grounds were sold off, the grounds became neglected. Mrs Tom Jones Evans from Dinchope went along and removed the horseshoe gravestone that had been covered in weeds and erected it alongside Grove Sprightly's at Dinchope.

Although the Lords of Corfton Manor in the C16 were the Foxe family of Bromfield, the Baldwyns and Stedmans also owned much of the Corfton lands. The Baldwyns slowly accumulated their land holding by purchasing the Foxe's land. In 1779, the Baldwyns sold their Corfton lands to Wilson Aylesbury Roberts of Bewdley, whose descendants went on to build Corfton Hall.

Corfton Hall - Shropshire.

Corfton Hall was a warm red brick patterned house accompanied by Grinshill stone. It was built by Thomas Lloyd Roberts in 1875, in similar Jacobean style, to nearby Lutwyche Hall and they were both designed by the Munslow - born architect, Samuel Pountney Smith. Corfton Hall was a large house with thirteen bedrooms as well as six more for servants. An elaborate stable for eleven horses was built alongside and it was surrounded by 17 acres of park and garden. Edward Wood of Culmington bought it in 1889 after Thomas Lloyd Robert's death and it was rented out until it was sold again in 1911. The new owner was Percy Giles Holder who owned 4560 acres, including several farms and houses in the Corvedale. He sold the Hall in 1942 to the Church Commissioners. WWII saw the Women's Land Army move in and later the hall was used as an Agricultural Training Board hostel. It was demolished, except for the Lodge and the stables in 1948. The author once lived at the bungalow built alongside the site of the hall in 1967.

C17 Corfton, Sun Inn with its petrol pumps on the opposite side of the Corvedale road. The garage was first opened by Sidney Cadwallader in the 1930s and the sign tells us that petrol was costing 1s 5d a gallon. Known as the Sun since 1758, it was first licensed in 1770 when John Maebury was landlord. In 1901 the Sun was owned by Edward Wood of Culmington Manor and Edwin Cox was the landlord.

This is a rare invoice from the Sun Inn, sent to Benjamin Flounder, in 1833. It shows two dinners at eleven shillings each, wine fifteen shillings, spirits four shillings and two pence, tobacco sixpence, ale and cider seventeen shillings and six pence, hay and corn three shillings and six pence. The total is five pounds, five shillings and two pence when the hardworking servants had to manage on two shillings and six pence!

A very famous young lady named Molly Jones lived with her parents in a cottage behind the Sun Inn. She was baptised in Diddlebury church on 31st January, 1762. Her father was a rabbit catcher and also worked part time at the Sun. In 1778, Molly went out to work at William Gough's Lower House Farm. Five years later she had a baby girl that was presumed to be William Gough's. In 1785 she married William Morgan, who worked as a carpenter for Thomas Pinches at Bach Mill. Molly had a son and she moved, with William and the two children, to Cold Weston. In 1789 she and her husband, were accused of stealing hemp from behind the Sun Inn. Both were

To R. DYER. Sun Inn, Corfton. Oct 2nd 1833	£	s.	D.
Breakfast			
Lunch			
Dinner 2/ each	1	2	..
Tea			
Supper			
Wine	2	15	.
Spirits		4	2
Punch			
Tobacco			6
Ale and Cider		17	6
Bed			
Hay and Corn		3	6
Grass			
Servants' Eating and Ale		2	6
£	5	5	2

arrested but William escaped and Molly tried to cut her throat whilst imprisoned at the Sun. She was found guilty and sentenced to death but the sentence was later altered to fourteen years transportation to Australia. A four month ship journey saw a third of the 502 convicts die but Molly survived by being nice to the captain and was allowed to be on top deck during the journey. Mysteriously, her husband William joined her in Parramatta, Australia where they kept a shop. She missed her children back home and escaped in 1794 on a ship bound for England. She met and married Thomas Mears of Plymouth but was accused of setting fire to his house after an argument and she left him. In 1803 she stole some clothing and was sent back to Australia for seven years. She had her sentence extended by another seven years for stealing government cattle. In 1822 aged 61 she married again to Thomas Hood aged 31! Molly bought land and became a well respected citizen, helping to build a church and a school. She was a grafter and could dig drains, build fences and dams better than most men. She built up a fortune opening hotels, but at the age of 73, she died alone and with a mortgage on her last and only property. Several hotels and vineyards are named after her and she is still remembered as the Queen of Hunter Valley.

CORFTON.

The Sun Inn and garage.

In 1940, Morris Barker & Poole sold the Sun Inn on behalf of the owner, Mrs Cadwallader. The new owner was Mr Shallcross of East Lothian, Scotland who paid £3.010 for the Sun Inn, farm buildings, garage, petrol pumps and 20 acres of pasture. In 1944, the landlord Walter Cole ran the garage next door in the old outbuildings and he was there from 1944 until 1972. The Sun is at present kept by the Pearce family and has been so since 1984. Norman Pearce opened up a brewery in a building at the rear of the Inn in 1997 and has won several awards for his real ale brews.

Corfton Estate cottages.

The 31 neo–Tudor style cottages on the Corfton estate were restored, two each year, from 1854, by Thomas Lloyd Roberts. They were and, still are, very picturesque with their leaded casements and ornamental barge boards.

Corfton Castle mound.

Corfton Castle, alias 'the Mound', is high up at the Hill House Farm where the Pugh family have farmed for many years. You can see the remaining mound where the C12 castle sat and the farmhouse beyond.

Corfton Chapel.
Besides a castle, at Hill House, there was St Bartholomew's chapel, originally built in the C13 and rebuilt in the C17 by a man who did not want to go to the parish church. It is now used as an agricultural building.

Charles Pugh from Hill House Farm, Corfton, tedding hay, with Hill House, the chapel and castle mound in the background.

Victory Motorcycle Trials.
Sid Caddick could not resist taking this photo of the unfortunate motor cyclist taking a spill during the motor cycle trails held annually throughout the Corvedale. Notice the soldiers on leave from WWII.

Caddick's Stores at Corfton showing an array of assorted items for sale. The author supplied the shop with fruit and vegetables in the early 1960s and remembers how well the Caddick shop was thought of by its customers.

Corvedale lorry crash.
Sid Caddick met Crowther's lorry at Lower Corfton and came off worst. That did not stop him getting a photo of the accident. Luckily no one was hurt!

Sun Cottage, over the road from the Sun Inn at Corfton. This was one of thirty one Corfton estate cottages that were rebuilt by Thomas Lloyd Roberts when he inherited the estate in 1854.

The meandering river Corve, getting wider and much appreciated by the livestock.

The mobile cider press at Corfton.
Apples were brought to the press by smallholders and farmers from the area to make their very own cider.

Upper Corfton showing some of the Corfton Estate houses.

What a gem of a picture! **'Bait time in the Corvedale'.**

Moving on down the B4368 towards Craven Arms, we find the roadmen at 'bait time' on Wheelers Oak bank, just prior to Pedlars Rest in 1938. Traffic was more a rarity than today and that is why Mr Clee and Titch Luscott were sitting in the road. In the 1800s 'a lengthsman', employed by Ludlow Highways Board, was responsible to the Waywarden who was responsible to the Surveyor of the Highway Board, later to become the Rural District Council. In 1885 there were fourteen lengthsmen employed in the Corvedale, each man had a set length of highway which he cared for. The Waywarden was a local man who knew the area and farmers well and would ensure the adjoining trees, hedges, ditches and drains were kept tidy.

The junction at Pedlars Rest on the B4368. The house by the signpost was the old turnpike house built in the early C19 and was demolished in the 1980s. Straight on, is Craven Arms, turn left, towards Culmington and Ludlow. Over the hedge to the left is a damson tree that stands over an empty tomb with iron railings around a four ton slab of granite. Its story will be revealed later (see Elsich Manor picture).

Carrying on down the B4368 towards Craven Arms is Seifton and, after a right turn off the B4368, is Seifton Batch.

The first building at Seifton Batch is the **Primitive Methodist Chapel,** also known as Golden Plackett Chapel. It was built of stone with polychrome brick dressings in 1874 and closed in the 1950s. It is now a private residence.

Seifton Batch.

As you can see on this Caddick photo, Seifton Batch is an idyllic valley with a slow pace of life – if the gentleman in the picture is anything to go by.

Seifton Batch.

There are fourteen houses in the Batch and the picture shows how deep the valley is, making it a quite isolated spot.

Harriet James/nee Bright.

This wonderful old lady was born on Valentine's day 1816. She is Harriet Bright and she was baptised at Ludlow on 11th February, 1821. She worked for farmer Richard Davies at New House Farm, Sibdon Carwood in 1841. Harriet married Richard James from Aldon in 1842 at Stokesay church and they had six children. She worked as a farmhand, moving from Brand Hill, Onibury to Seifton and then to Turnpike Road, Diddlebury by 1881. She was a widow living at Seifton Batch by 1911. She moved to Ludlow workhouse and enjoyed her 100th birthday on February 14th 1916. Harriet's fellow inmates wished to provide a birthday party, but this was refused by the workhouse governors due to the ten shilling cost.

Harriet James's grave.

Harriet died on October 12th, 1916 aged 100 and was buried in Culmington churchyard, east of the church, the funeral costs being borne by a friend. She had witnessed a century of change in the Corvedale, bringing up six children and working as a farmhand, which would not have been an easy life. She lived during the life and times of six monarchs and thirty four prime ministers. Born during the reign of George III, followed by George IV, then William IV, Queen Victoria, Edward VII and George V. She would have seen the first motor cars, railways and aeroplanes. Although in 2012 there were about 13,000 people in Britain aged 100, in 1916 there were only 100. Well done Harriet! It looks as if the Corvedale was a healthy place to live in.

Milford Lodge.

Built in the Regency period, around 1821, Milford Lodge stands high up on the northern side of the B4368. It was built for the Downes family, as a gentleman farmer's residence, with 28 acres. Almost certainly, Milford Lodge was the first property in the area to have gas installed for heating and lighting. One of the outbuildings housed an acetylene generating plant in the late 1800s. Jeremiah Downes, from the Grange at Leintwardine, had inherited Aston Hall, New House, Broadstone Mill and Club Farm from his brother Thomas in 1801. He resided at Aston Hall until his death in 1809. Jeremiah's son, Thomas and his wife Mary went to live at Milford Lodge from Aston Hall. Thomas died there aged 60, in 1849 and Mary in 1877 aged 89. Thomas's nephew, Arthur Henry Downes, was born at Milford Lodge in 1851 and was later knighted for his research into health and disease. He ended his days in Mount Carmel, Haifa, Palestine, where the Sir Arthur Downes Library was opened in his memory in 1939. It houses his 1400 books that were presented to the British Sailors Society, Princess Royal Institute, Haifa. A plaque reads: To the memory of Sir Arthur Downes MD:

HE WAS A MAN OF SCIENCE,
EVER SEEKING TRUTH, KNOWLEDGE AND UNDERSTANDING
TO THE LAST HOUR OF HIS LONG LIFE,
CLOSING 11TH MARCH 1938
AT HIS HOUSE
AT "LA DOUNE, MOUNT CARMEL.

Tower House, Burley.

The hamlet of Burley, in Culmington parish, was so named after the family of William de Burley who resided at Broncroft Castle in the C15. The Tower House is a three storey castellated house which was built as a folly by Benjamin Flounders who owned the Culmington Estate in the early C19.

Bishop Brothers of Burley, Les and Cyril and Percy, were fanatical about steam engines and they not only used them in their work up until the 1960s but they restored steam engines for several others owners.

Bishops of Burley's yard.

Bishops held an annual fair at their yard at Burley for the locals and were co-instigators of the 1961 Church Stretton Steam Fair (to become the Bishops Castle Steam Fair in 1970) which moved to Walcot Hall, Lydbury North in 1991, and is, since 1994, the County of Salop Steam Engine Society at Onslow Park near Shrewsbury.

Selina Lane outside her home at Vernolds Common in 1915.

Selina is on the left with her niece Polly on the right. Selina Lane was mistress at Vernolds Common School for over twenty years despite having a disability that forced her to use crutches. At the age of eighteen months she fell, dislocated her hip and injured her spine. Because she could not explain her feelings, her injuries were not understood until it was too late. Her right leg was paralysed and she had a leg iron on the left leg. Selina was a very highly regarded mistress and loved by her pupils. Her niece, Polly, was housekeeper for Selina, Selina's father and Selina's brother Mark Lane.

Selina Lane with Verolds Common school children and niece Polly on right.
The infant school was built in 1874 and was the property of Herbert John Allcroft of Stokesay Court. The average attendance was ten pupils in 1909 but it looks as if the attendance had grown dramatically when this photo was taken around 1920.

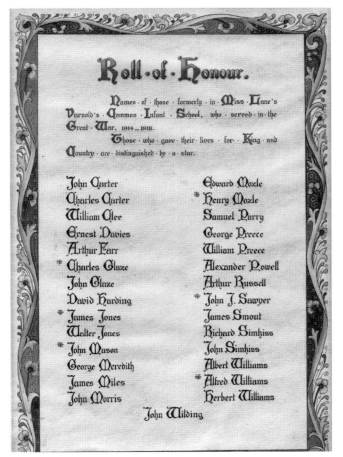

Roll of Honour.

Names of those formerly in Miss Lane's Varnold's Common Infant School, who served in the Great War, 1914–1918.

Those who gave their lives for King and Country are distinguished by a star.

John Carter	Edward Mozle
Charles Carter	* Henry Mozle
William Clee	Samuel Parry
Ernest Davies	George Preece
Arthur Farr	William Preece
* Charles Glaze	Alexander Powell
John Glaze	Arthur Russell
David Harding	* John J. Sawyer
* James Jones	James Smout
Walter Jones	Richard Simkiss
* John Mason	John Simkiss
George Meredith	Albert Williams
James Miles	* Alfred Williams
John Morris	Herbert Williams
John Wilding	

Vernolds Common Roll of Honour.

This scroll was hung in the school, showing Selina Lane's pupils that served in WW1. The five stars indicate those who failed to return.

119

Richard Simkiss.

One that did return was Richard Simkiss, he came back to his wife Emily and they kept a smallholding at Whettleton Hill, Stokesay.

Richard and Mary Anne Lane
pictured at No. 35 Vernolds Common circa 1920.

Richard was born at Farlow in 1849 and moved to Vernolds Common area c.1880, no doubt following sister Selina. He married Mary Anne Rollings at Culmington in 1881 and they had 9 children. Richard died in 1924 and Mary Anne moved to Ludlow with her daughter Mary. Richards's son, Richard, then moved into No.35 and he died in 1975.

Mark Lane,
brother to Selina Lane.

Mark, seen here mending quarry trucks at Onibury quarry, near to the railway crossing. He lost one leg in an accident at the age of eleven. He was the father of Miss Rose Lane who became Mrs Cecil Crowther.

Vernolds Common at the Lane family home showing Culmington rector, Rev David Erskine Holland with Selina Lane. Back row – George Parry, Rose Lane, Albert Lane, Nell Jones, Frank Davies, Bessie Jones. Front row – Ned Parry and two 'unknown'.

Miss Rose Lane aged eighteen resting in the grounds of Stokesay Court where she was a house maid.

Mrs Rotton of Stokesay Court holding the young tree. The young girl with the spade is Miss Jewell Allcroft and they are celebrating Jewell's coming of age on September 15th 1928. Stokesay Court was built by John Derby Allcroft who was a Victorian merchant, philanthropist, social Conservative, Christian Evangelist and church builder (1822-1893). His father Jeremiah Allcroft was a partner of Dent brothers, the glove makers at London in 1822. They opened a factory in Worcester. By 1855 the Dent brothers and Jeremiah had retired and John Derby Allcroft became Managing Director. He was a very shrewd man and by 1884 he had quadrupled production, producing twelve million pairs of gloves a year, which made the company the leading glove manufacturer in the world. John bought the Stokesay Court estate which was of considerable size, and comprised of Stokesay Castle, Stoke Wood, Whettleton, Aldon, Newton, Onibury, Stepaside, Burley, Walton, and Duxmoor, in the parishes of Stokesay, Onibury and Culmington. The total area was 5,200 acres with an annual rental of £7,000 in 1869.

In 1874, John also bought the Stone House estate in Aldon Parish, the home of Lady Mary Ann Syer. He wanted to settle down and Stokesay Castle was unsuitable to live in but the Stone House was too small so he called in the architect Thomas Harris and work started on building Stokesay Court in 1889 and it was finished in 1892. The area where he wanted to build his house was not for sale from the lady owner so he waited until she died and bought it off her son. It lay between his two estates. No expense was spared – under floor heating in the great hall and electricity installed by Edmondsons in 1891. Sadly John Derby Allcroft died just six months after completion. John's son and heir took over. He put the finishing touches to the Court and gardens were laid out in 1892 by E H Milner. A lake, fountain, plant houses and grotto were developed.

Stokesay Court during World War I.
The Court was used as an Auxiliary Military Hospital for convalescence. It was again used as a Military hospital in WWII. It was also occupied for a year by Lancing College when they were evacuated from Sussex, and then became a Western Command Junior Leaders School.

John Derby Allcroft's grandchildren, Russell and Jewel, lived at the Court until 1994. The Court is now the home of Caroline Magnus, niece of Jewell Magnus Allcroft.

Rose Lane at her wedding to Cecil Crowther.
Cecil was from off the Clee Hill and was used to a hard working life. He would not have known, at this time, that he would soon become the boss of a haulage company employing several drivers.

G. C. Crowther's haulage yard at Medley Park in 1961.

You could not travel far without meeting a Crowther's lorry in the 1960s and 1970s. Lorries were contracted to the council, lorries delivered and spread lime for farmers, hauled building materials and carried out general haulage. If you wanted something moving, Crowther's were the firm to call.

G. C. Crowther's Annual works party in 1979.

As you can see the company had flourished and had a good compliment of drivers. The picture shows drivers and wives enjoying their party with Cecil and Rose Crowther with their three sons and their wives on the front row – Derek and Olive, Martin and Heather, Cecil and Rose, Clive and Rose.

Vernolds Common Chapel.

Besides running his haulage business, Cecil Crowther was a lay preacher at Vernolds Common Non Conformist Methodist Chapel. The chapel was built of stone in 1858, and was well used by local folk in the sparsely populated area.

Vernolds Common Chapel Party.

The chapel was well attended and parties were held for the local children. Sadly times changed and the chapel closed in 1997. It has been converted into a residence and has a plaque on the wall commemorating its former use.

Vernolds Common Chapel Outing.

Cecil and Rose Crowther with helpers Olive Crowther and Mr and Mrs George Dawson, taking care of the Vernolds Common children on their annual trip to somewhere special.

School Transport.

The children from Vernolds Common and surrounding hamlets were transported to Onibury school by the education bus. Here they are waiting for Bernard Baker the driver. Several of the children are of the Smallman family, cousins of the author.

Bert Lane of Vernolds Common pictured in 1947 on his 350 Aerial, at the entrance to Culmington Manor. Transport was essential for Vernolds Common folk for getting to work in the nearby towns. Bert worked at Farmore Mills, Craven Arms for many years.

Sixteen year old Nora Thomas outside her home at the Thatches, Vernolds Common in 1926.
This young lady is the author's mother who was about to leave home for her new work as a nippy at Lyons Corner House in London. Quite a change!

Corvedale Valley.
Whilst stopping briefly to look around, you will find the views in the Corvedale absolutely stunning. It shows the lush valley fields and the hills surrounding the valley, ideal for producing fine, strong lambs.

Elsich Manor.
Elsich Manor is thought to have been built by Richard Baldwyn II of Diddlebury for his son William in 1545 and the Baldwyn family remained there until Charles Baldwyn, MP for Ludlow, leased Stokesay Castle from the Earl of Craven in 1635. Elsich was then leased to tenants, who included John Walcot of

Walcot in 1657. Mr Drake of the 12th Light Dragoons married a young lady aged 22, from Elsich, in 1807. She accompanied the regiment to the battle of Waterloo on 18th June, 1815 and was present during the great battle for eight hours as a nurse, assisting the doctors attending the wounded. The immensity of the battle is hard to comprehend! The 12th Light Dragoons lost 6 officers and 106 men in the battle. In total, Wellington lost 15,000 dead or wounded and Blucher of the Prussian army another 7,000. Napoleon lost 25,000 dead or wounded with 8,000 taken prisoner. Mrs Drake stayed on throughout the whole Peninsular campaign and lived to reach the age of 100. In 1779 Wilson Aylesbury Roberts bought Elsich and leased it out to several tenants until it was purchased in 1911, with 475 acres, for £10,300, by P. G. Holder, outbidding the tenant Edward Edwards. Edward eventually bought Elsich and bequeathed it to his son Charles Edward Edwards.

Charles, in his lifetime was to become a farmer, auctioneer, race horse owner, breeder and trainer. Charlie, as he was known, was born at Abbey farm, Hawkestone in north Shropshire on August 13th 1872.

Charlie Edwards at Ellesmere College 1884.

Charlie attended the local school at Weston until he was twelve, when he entered Ellesmere College. He was the son of a farming family and, in 1891, at the young age of eighteen, he loaned £200 from his

father to immigrate to Canada, to try his hand at farming on his own. He bought 160 acres at Calgary for just ten dollars, bought 300 sheep at one dollar each, built a log cabin and remained there for the next four years, until his father recalled him to farm at the family farm in Shropshire. Charlie had been successful and, in 1895, he sold his 160 acres for £650, sold off his cattle, sheep and horses and returned home with the £200 to repay the loan and £1,000 in his pocket. His father had moved his farming interests to 475 acres in the Corvedale at Elsich Manor, Culmington, South Shropshire. Charlie lived at Elsich until 1914 when he built and moved to Mount Seifton Farm near to Elsich Manor. His father turned over the farm at Elsich to Charlie which made him a large scale farmer, now married with one son and five daughters.

Charlie Edwards (with gun under the arm), overseeing his workmen lugging in the root crop with four teams of horse and cart. Charlie became a well respected farmer who regularly fought the corner for his fellow farmers, especially against the government. He believed that government interfered too much and tried to teach farmers their job from behind city desks. *(Nothing has changed)*. Charlie soon became known as a top breeder of both sheep and cattle and was reputed to be one of the finest judges of cattle, sheep and horses in the U.K. His fondest love was the horse.

Three generations of the Edwards family.

Charlie was a top flight horseman and noted horse breeder, bringing all his family up with the same outlook. This picture shows Charlie with his children and grand children at the Christmas Meet of the hounds at his home at Mount Seifton in 1949. Charlie's five daughters and son Ken, at the tender age of five, took first prize for the family event at Meifod show in mid Wales. One daughter rode at Ludlow Point to Point at only thirteen years of age.

In 1947 Charlie won the Kings Cup at Epsom with his stallion 'Timur'.
Charlie's winner's cups numbered well over one hundred. He was proud that he had sold horses to the King of England and even one that our present Queen Elizabeth rode. Charlie joined the Shropshire Yeomanry and was soon a sergeant and became champion swordsman of the company as his father had been years earlier. One of his Yeomanry highlights was in 1914 when he escorted King George V on his visit to the Royal Show, held in Shrewsbury. Charlie tried his hand at politics in 1944, standing as an Independent candidate for the Ludlow Division of Shropshire and in 1946 he stood as a National Independent in the Salop County Council Elections. He lost his deposit and £3,000 but he had tried. The author, when only seven years old, can recall standing by a bran tub stand with no money to 'have a go' at Culmington Manor Fete in the late 1940s. Charlie came up, dressed in his ten gallon hat and racoon coat, pressing sixpence into the delighted boy's hand so that he could pull out a present from the bran tub. A moment that has never been forgotten by the author.

Charlie Edwards.
Things did not always go Charlie's way and after an altercation with the War Agricultural Committee he was committed to prison for refusing to pay his £20 fine. His sentence was reduced from two months to two weeks because they found £18.13s.7p in his pockets. He refused to add a couple of pounds to the amount and said he wanted to serve his sentence, which he did.

CHARLES EDWARD EDWARDS.
BORN AT ABBY FARM. HAWKESTONE
13. AUG. 1872.

FOR THE LORD'S SAKE
WORK AS HARD AS YOU CAN.
LIVE AS LONG AS YOU CAN.
DO ALL THE GOOD YOU CAN
TO ALL THE PEOPLE YOU CAN.

Charlie was a forward thinking man. Years before his death he ordered his coffin and built his tombstone with railings around, situated in a field on the parish boundary at Mount Seifton. He wanted his head to be in Diddlebury parish and his feet in Culmington parish so that he could keep watch on his workmen. On hearing this, the shepherd remarked, *"we'll bury thee face down'ards"*. The coffin was ordered and when it arrived in a black van he asked if he could see his future home. He was shown a beautiful, polished oak coffin with brass handles. On his death in 1954 he was not allowed to be buried there.

After such a strenuous and active career, you would have thought that he would have wanted to retire in peace at the age of seventy five, but not Charlie. He was approached by several breeders' societies to represent them abroad to highlight the quality of British breeding stock and perhaps sell stock to the foreign buyers. He must have been overjoyed at the request; it was an acknowledgment from the breeding societies of his superb skill of negotiating and his tremendous knowledge of animals and the value of them. He set off on 30th January, 1948; he went around the world using boat and aeroplane, arriving back in Liverpool on 30th July, 1948.

Charlie Edwards in Egypt.

Charlie's trip around the world was an experience and very successful. In Madrid he sold 2,000 horses, 50 registered stallions, 200 boar pigs and 100 Cheviot rams to the Spanish government and that was a smaller order than the one placed by the Egyptian government. Charlie was certainly a strong willed character who stood his corner and lived life to the full. He passed away in 1954. His two grandsons (sons of Charlie's son Ken), Colin and Robin live at Mount Seifton and nearby Medley Park.

Following the B4365 from Elsich towards Ludlow, next comes the village of Culmington.

All Saints - Culmington

Culmington Church.

C11 All Saints Church at Culmington is one of the oldest churches in Shropshire. Several additions and alterations were carried out in 1865 and 1969. There are two fonts; one Victorian and one Norman dating from 1150 AD. The latter came from Burwarton Church which is now closed. There are wall paintings from the C17 and a rood screen from the C15. The wooden spire indicates that the money ran out by the time they got to building it. There are three C17 bells and seating for 200. An epitaph in the churchyard reads:

Good natured, generous, bold and free
He always was in company.
He loved his bottle and his friend
Which brought on soon his latter end.

Three Culmington vicars died of the Black Plague between 1346 and 1349. Also in the churchyard, near to the church, there is a cockerel engraved on a stone. It is said that the old squire, who was buried here, used to regularly shoot at the weathercock on the church. On the night he was buried, there was a storm and the wind blew the weathercock down and it landed on top of the squire's grave. To record this incident, the stonemason carved the image of the cockerel in one corner of the squire's headstone.

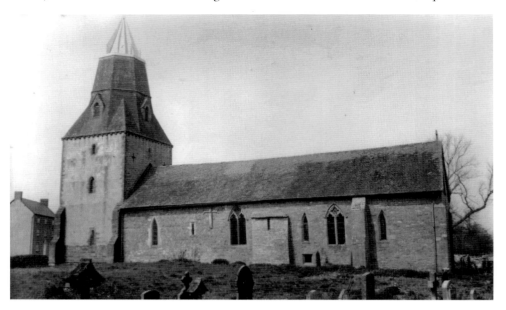

Culmington Church.

A more recent postcard showing the modern aluminium spire. Local rumour has it that the spire was erected with the aid of a helicopter in 1969 but, after an investigation by the author, he believes it was hauled up piece by piece on a pulley and welded together.

Culmington Church spire.

This photo shows builder Mr Tom Perkins of Little Brampton who, with the help of Brian Robinson of Broome, hauled up the parts for the spire using the pulley seen on the left. Once complete, the aluminium spire was fixed to a metal frame in the roof.

Culmington Church interior.

The centre window on the south side of the nave is to the memory of Captain Gordon Wood from Culmington Manor who was killed in the South African Boer War in 1900. In 1902, oak choir stalls were installed in memory of Queen Victoria. The single manual organ came from Aconbury church that had been closed and was installed in Culmington church in 1974. A refurbishment of the organ took place in 2012.

The Royal Oak at Culmington was a very busy village inn and had been since 1830. It contained a tap room, kitchen, parlour, sitting room, five bedrooms and stabling for two horses. The Anslow family kept the inn and the adjoining blacksmith's shop, followed by Thomas Lawley. Thomas split the businesses by 1905 when Charles Beeks took over the blacksmith's shop. John William Holt was landlord in 1913, followed by Douglas Robertson in 1922 until 1941. Arthur Howes was landlord in 1955, followed by John Sutton. The last landlord for four years before it was closed was Roger Dunn. It was then converted into a private house by the Lines family.

Sparchford Farm.

Sparchford was once a small hamlet but all that remains today is Sparchford Farm and Sparchford Cottage. A farmhouse has stood there since the mid C16 with several well-to-do owners including Sir Charles Foxe of Bromfield in the C16, James Lacon in the C18 and Benjamin Flounders in the C19. Charlie Edwards from Mount Seifton bought Sparchford farm in 1911 for £8,000. It was then described as "an C18 farmhouse with earlier interior". The Burgoyne family farmed the land and ran a contracting business from Sparchford for several years. The Jones family bought the farm in the 1950s and remain there today, farming and running a camp site.

From little acorns.

Tucked away at Sparchford is an abattoir where Caines, (a family run business) has operated for many years. It all started in 1919 when Michael Caine saw the need for someone to collect casualty animals from the surrounding farms. He would take his horse and cart to collect sheep, cows and horses and process them into animal food. He started at Longville and moved to Culmington in the 1930s. The business grew and there are now four depots with lorries covering a radius of some 100 miles. From a horse and cart collection in 1919 to a fleet of lorries that have a computerised lorry tracking system and new online stock history service is quite an achievement.

Grade II listed Culmington House is of the Queen Anne style with 7 bedrooms, 5 bathrooms and 4 reception rooms. Standing in over 4 acres, with a cottage in the well laid out gardens, the Prince Phillimore School of English was here until 1995 when it reverted back into a private residence. It is currently for sale for £1.4 million.

Culmington House Garden.
Lt Colonel Stephen Henry Worrall DSO lived at Culmington House for three decades from 1909 and he is seen here in the walled garden. In 1914 he presented the village with a new reading room.

The Cottage, Culmington.

The original postcard was sent by this lady relaxing in the garden at her home – 'The Cottage' at Culmington in 1905. She writes, "I have come, house and all, to wish you a merry Christmas and perhaps five brace. S. E. Bowen". Charles B. Overton, the Culmington tax collector, moved into the cottage in 1929.

Culmington Village.

A Caddick postcard, shows the lovely B&W house in Culmington. The village throughout the years has had a pub, blacksmith, laundry, post office, grocer, wheelwright, school and tailor, all of which have disappeared. What is still in the village is a very well supported village Hall, built in 1997.

The Church of England National mixed School at Culmington, was built in 1857 with residence for the master. It was enlarged in 1879 for 93 children and the average attendance was 70. This picture shows pupils with master and mistress in 1937. The school closed and the building has been used since then to house a pottery business.

Noel Leslie Good 1915–1992.

Noel lived at Aston Munslow before moving to his new bungalow at Culmington. He was a very busy man. He cared for his woodland at Wall under Heywood, including growing Christmas trees for the retail trade. He was an early riser and would deliver the local and national newspapers every day on a sixty mile a day delivery round.

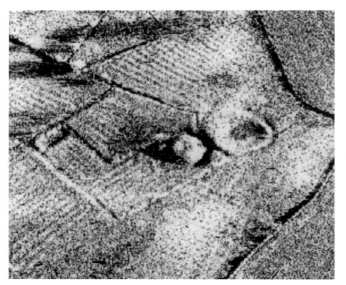

Culmington Camp Ring.

Culmington is located in lower Corvedale and contains the magnificent remains of a motte and bailey castle known as 'Camp Ring'. There are no known surviving medieval references to either its history or owners. It stands on a low ridge above water-meadows between the River Corve and Pye Brook. The circular motte is just over two metres in height and is surrounded by a ditch which would have possibly been filled with water. An attached further bailey is fifty metres in diameter and is enclosed by a five metre wide bank and outer ditch.

Culmington Manor was built in 1854 and included a 100 acre park with a lodge at each of the two entrances. It was the home of Edward Wood of Ealing, London, from 1874 and his family lived there until the 1940s. His family had mining businesses in the Midlands before they moved to Ealing. They built Hanger Hill house at Ealing and accumulated 900 acres of very precious land and properties which they kept after Edward's retirement. Much of the land was later bought up by railway companies and, in 1906, Edward sold 850 houses to the Prudential for £250,000. In 1920 he sold Hanger Hill house and land to develop a golf course. The only thing the Wood family left at Ealing were the street names such as Culmington Road, Corfton Road, Craven Road, Woodfield Road and, one named after his wife, Boileau Road.

Culmington Manor later became the home of John Herbert Mallet Shaw and Mrs Shaw. Today Culmington Manor is the home of Manor Adventure which has been offering activities for school children since 1992. Hidden away in the Corvedale Valley, the estate provides a safe and secure environment for schools to enjoy outdoor pursuits.

Sid Lawley was born at Holdgate in 1894. He signed up for military service at Craven Arms in Aug 1914. Twice wounded in France, he spent a total of 6 months in hospital. Despite his injuries causing restricted movement in some of his fingers he went on to captain Culmington cricket team and play football for Craven Arms. He once had a trial for Shrewsbury Town. It is quite a coincidence that he has a spade to play with, because he would have not known that in later life he would work as a gardener at Culmington Manor and, later Culmington House, for Colonel Worrall. He retired to Church Stretton where he died in 1975.

Seifton Court.
Grade II listed, Seifton Court, once named The Home Farm, is a C17 period farmhouse situated in Seifton, Culmington. It was the home of the Humphries family for over seventy years during the C20 and was a working farm with a B & B business.

Lawton farm.

The Lawton estates were in the hands of the Baskerville family in the C13 until the C16, passing to the Lutley family until 1792 when it was sold to the Cornewall family of Diddlebury. In 1910, George William Hide bought Lawton from where he set up a racing stable. George's son, Eddie Hide, became a famous flat racing jockey, winning 2593 races during his successful career in the 1960s and 1970s. Edward's brother Anthony also became a successful jockey and his best win was the Thirsk Gold Cup. He became a trainer, moving to Italy in 1973 where he trained the winner of the 1974 Italian 2,000 guineas – Mannsfield. Lawton Farm was sold in 1976 to the Brick family from Knighton.

Eddie Hide.

Born in 1937, Eddie Hide started his riding career at the age 13, retiring at the age of 49. He rode 2593 winners including six classics. At his retirement he was sixth in the all time winners' list.

Lawton's shell hole being inspected during WWII. The bomb was dropped to lighten the German plane returning home to Germany after a bombing raid. Bert Lewis (centre).

Sutton Court was built in the early 1400's and owned by the Powell family from 1473. In 1764, Rev John Powell was absentee vicar of Pennington Lancashire and was also Curate of Diddlebury until 1803. He was a JP, using his home to hear cases, including committing Molly Morgan at Shrewsbury in 1789. He also officiated Molly's wedding and christened her two children. The last of the Powell family to live at Sutton Court was Lionel Powell who was a famous impresario and he died in 1931. It was sold to P.G. Holder for £12,000. He sold it on to the Church Commissioners in 1959 and they sold it to the Harvey family. Sir Lesley and Lady Sally Fielding lived there until 1998. During WWII the Court was taken over by the British Army. It was called the Government Laundry Service Depot to hide the real function of those based at the Court who were the Special Operations Executive - responsible for organising the drop of secret agents behind enemy lines and into Europe. Probably the bombs dropped at nearby Lawton were intended for the Court!

Sutton Court.

Lionel Powell (at the steering wheel) at his Sutton Court home in the early 1920s, surrounded by his musical friends, including famous pianist, Herr Pachmann.

Little Sutton.

It is thought that Little Sutton (now Sutton Court Farm) was the De Sutton home – the original manor before Sutton Court was built next door. Probably the original manor existed in the early C11. The addition of two wings with massive chimneys in the C16 is what you see today. Nearby was the C13 chapel of St George's which was demolished long ago. The Foxe family from Bromfield owned Great and Little Sutton from the mid C16. Both were sold to Henry, Lord Herbert in 1660, who sold them to Edward Baldwyn in 1709. In 1910 P.G. Holder became the owner followed by the Church Commissioners and lastly the Boyne estates. Several tenants farmed Little Sutton but in 1985 the house was separated from the land and sold to the Beaumont–Nesbitt family.

Great Sutton farm is a large rectangular building with timber framing forming square panels and dates about 1700. It was originally a plain building with the timber squares covered by a screed. A butcher, named William Millman, was trading from here in the 1890s.

Clee St Margaret Ford.

Caddick must have thought he was in heaven when he came upon this idyllic scene at Clee St Margaret ford. Clee brook runs through the village to form reputedly the longest ford in Shropshire at fifty metres long. The Clee brook then runs into the Pye brook and on into the river Corve.

Clee Liberty Common.

Clee St Margaret parish includes Clee Liberty Common. The common is around 540 acres of unspoilt land used by graziers and includes the Nordy Bank Iron Age Hill Fort which is a scheduled ancient monument. The man made earthwork and ditch ring can still be easily identified, even after two thousand five hundred years. The common is owned by the villagers, managed and maintained by the parish council and the commoners association.

Nordy Bank.

Primitive Methodist Camp Meetings were held throughout Shropshire. Hugh Bourne 1772-1852 and William Clowes were co-founders of the Primitive Methodists, an offshoot of the Wesleyan Methodists in 1807. As you can see, huge crowds gathered after trekking three miles up the hill. They mostly sang Moody or Sankey hymns. They usually had no accompanist, someone started singing and the rest followed. The meetings were held up until 1950 when the old followers had died and the young folk had other distractions like television and cinemas.

Hugh Bourne was born in Bucknall, Staffordshire and held his first Camp Meeting at Mow Cop on the Staffordshire-Cheshire border with an attendance of 4,000. His second meeting was on the Wrekin in Shropshire. He believed in equal status of men and women and appointed women preachers. Singing would play a large part of the meeting with a picnic to follow. After a camp meeting would follow a Love-Feast, ending with a prayer meeting. Several preachers would attend each meeting.

Richard Jukes 1804-1867, a stone mason from Goat Hill, Clungunford became a well sought after preacher in 1827, swelling congregations for thirty two years until his retirement. He married Phoebe Pardoe in 1825 but she died the following year of typhus. Richard then married Charlotte Smith and they had eight children. He also became a prolific hymn writer and poet. By 1860 Primitive Methodism had 650 ministers, 11,304 local preachers and over 100,000 members. The early 1900's saw a decline in membership and in 1932 the methodists united to keep the numbers up. Chapels would close for the day so that members could attend a meeting. Present times see only a few surviving open air circuit meetings.

REV. R. JUKES.

Clee St Margaret Village.

Historically, Clee St Margaret had a shop, five pubs, Methodist chapel, post office and a school, as in many other villages, they have all gone.

Miss Annie Childs ran the village shop in 1895 and was sub post mistress at the post office in the centre of the picture in 1900 until at least 1926. The house on the right is named the 'Steppes'.

Clee St Margaret Square.

Glebe farmhouse stands in the square where Wilfred Turner lived until 1952. The Heighway family followed and remained until 2001. Nordy Bank can be seen clearly in the background.

The church of St Margaret at Clee St Margaret is a Saxon/Norman build, dating back to the C11 and is now grade II listed. Notice the Saxon herring bone stonework, similar to Diddlebury church. 1871 saw a major restoration of the roof, floor, windows and installation of underground heating, the total cost being £388. John Clinton, a carpenter from Diddlebury restored the bellcote in 1878. A large yew tree fell on the church in 1980 which destroyed the vestry chimney and the roof had to be repaired.

The Vicarage, Clee St. Margaret, Shropshire.

WILDING'S SERIES 743.

Clee St Margaret vicarage was gifted by J.A.H. Thursby Pelham, the Lord of the Manor, at a cost of £1661. Rev Albert Clowes was the first vicar at the new vicarage in 1877. As you can see it was a grand building and the holding included 110 acres of glebe land. The Vicar at the time of this postcard was Rev Arthur John Knapton.

Clee St Margaret Vicarage in 1930.

Rev A.J. Knapton took this picture at the annual vicarage party. Mrs Knapton, his wife is third from the left on the back row. The children are from Abdon and Clee St Margaret School and the adults are teachers, school managers and helpers. Fourth from left on the back row is Mr Edwin Millichap, his wife Sophie is holding their daughter Beatrice, far right on the back row. Mr Millichap was the owner of the Clee Burf Stone Company.

Clee St Margaret School 1922.

The childrens' names (in no particular order) include: Ethel Clinton, Lucy Wear, Mary Weaver, Jane Hayhurst, Dolly Vaughan, Helen Hayhurst, Elsie Morgan, Cyril Turner, Harriet Banks, Margaret Banks, Hetty Wear, Bronco, Eddie Vaughan, Harold Weaver, Walter Heighway, Stan Heighway and Eddie Pheysey.

Clee Burf Stone Breaking Plant at Heathamgate 1925.

A stone crushing plant, known as 'The Cracker', needed about twenty five men to feed the stone into it and it was driven by a steam traction engine. The good quality, hard stone was ideal for road making and the sandstone was used for building. Among those present are: Sid Bennett, John Millichap, George Pheysey, George Bennett, Eddie Pheysey, Edwin Millichap, Harold Weaver and Walter Heighway.

Gwilt's Traction Engine, Clee St Margaret.

In 1930, Edwin Millichap,(with trilby behind the small boy in top picture), bought the stone company off Tom Gwilt from the Plough, opposite the quarry. He started excavating the dhu stone by hand; not using explosives and used Mr Southern's horses and drays to carry the stone down to the cracker at Heathamgate.

Heathamgate stone crushing plant.

Work was hard but pay was good, one shilling and six pence for every cubic yard of stone that was loaded on to a dray. Ten hours work was a normal day with saturday afternoon's off. The outbreak of WWII in 1939 brought the Clee Burf Quarry to a close.

Stoke St Milborough manor was settled by 1086, the earliest church was probably prior to the C12 and a mill was working in 1334. Wool and woollen cloth were the important products in the C14. In 1581, eleven tenants abandoned their holdings after a devastating storm period. In 1583, Oliver Briggs, son of Sir Humphrey Briggs, bought the Manor of Stoke St Milborough from Sir Thomas Smyth for £416. The deal included a mill, twenty farms, 10,000 acres of pasture, 100 acres of woodland, 200 acres of arable land, 500 acres of meadow and 4,000 acres of moor land. Not a bad buy! The Briggs family never lived in the area but the Manor remained in their family until 1767. The Lord of the Manor owned ironstone and limestone mines that he let to tenants. Limestone was being quarried at Stoke manor in 1637. The population of Stoke in 1815 was 554 but by 1991 it was down to around 300. On the edge of the parish, where it meets Hopton Cangeford and Cold Weston parishes, there is a stone cottage named the Scirmage that appears to be a one acre extra parochial parish of its own. This cottage is where a midwife delivered illegitimate babies from 1780 until at least 1805. Joceph Lycett a master forger, working from his home at Corve Street, Ludlow, sent Mary Stokes there to have her first child, Mary Ann Lycett in 1805. He was caught in 1811 forging bank notes and transported to Australia for fourteen years. He became famous for his detailed paintings of Australia, especially depicting the indigenous Aborigines' way of life. He was pardoned in 1821 and returned to Birmingham, England. He could not resist using his devious skills and was caught forging Stourbridge Bank notes. Rather than being sent back to Australia he cut his throat. While recuperating in hospital he tore open the healing wound and died aged fifty three, in 1828.

The Rectory, Stoke St. Milburgh-Shropshire.

WILDING'S SERIES 737

The Rectory at Stoke St Milborough was the home of Rev Harold John Chandos Burton in 1909 at the time of this photo. It had 70 acres of glebe land attached. The Rectory was positioned near to the church and boasted ten bedrooms and five reception rooms. It was remodelled in 1813 when a new drive, grotto, shrubbery and garden were added. The fish pool pre dates 1813 and suggests a much earlier rectory.

Stoke St Milborough Mill.

Charles, Bright and William Marston, were brothers and the operators of Stoke St Milborough water driven mill in 1900, followed by William Meredith in 1913.

The Lodge, Stoke St Milborough.

Edmund Hemming Owen, whose family had moved from Albrighton, built Stoke St Milburgh Lodge in the 1840s. He sold it along with his entire estate to Lord Boyne of Burwarton in 1867. At the time of this photo in 1909, the resident was Hon. Eustace Scott Hamilton-Russell JP. It was owned by his father F.G. Hamilton Russell, Lord of the Manor and chief landowner, who also owned Moor Hall.

Stoke St Milburgh church has stood in one form or another since at least the C12 and probably earlier. It was named after Milburga, a daughter of Merewald, King of part of Mercia, who founded the Abbey of Much Wenlock in the C7. Several restorations have been carried out through the centuries; in the C15 there were additions and alterations. In 1700 there was a major restoration and other restorations in 1859 and 1911. The tower contains eight bells, one from 1622 and three from 1637, two from 1773 and two from 1999. The rectangular churchyard was extended in 1898 and again in 1962.

Stoke St Milborough Primitive Methodist Chapel was erected in 1842. An average attendance in 1851 was 40 in the afternoon and 50 in the evening. A restoration was carried out in 1872 and the chapel served the community well until it ceased services in 1972. It has now been converted to a self catering luxury holiday home.

Stoke St Milborough School.

The first known school at Stoke St Milborough was built in 1760 and closed in 1820. It was revived in 1835 with twenty one fee paying pupils and by 1851 it had become a National school. The last school (pictured) was built in 1856 as a Public Elementary mixed school for eighty four children. The master was Arthur J. Slack. In the 1930s the master and his wife provided school meals. In 1941, fifteen evacuees from Liverpool were admitted. In 1958 children aged eleven were transferred to Ludlow C.E. Secondary Modern School. By 1968 the attendance was down to eighteen and the school was closed in 1969.

This is a postcard of the **Stoke St Milborough school children in 1923** with their teacher Miss West. The headmaster, not on the picture, was Albert Edward Worth.

Back row: George Harris, Jack Jones, Bill Roden, John Radmore, Horace Bullock.
Middle row: Lily Amphlett, Mary Lane, Nelly Price, Melba Moore, Lydia Jones, Molly Morris.
Front row: Violet Mellings, Alan Jones, Edna Jones, Dick Thomas, Gwen Meredith.
Sitting in front: Harold Mantle, Donald Radmore.

St. Mildburg's (or St. Milburgha's) well. A spring with an old stone basin, on the east side of Stoke village, was mentioned in 1321. It was later a common clothes-washing place. Stories of a miraculous origin were recorded in the mid 19th century, when the water was said to be good for sore eyes. It was covered in and altered in1873 and again in 1906. By 1945 its water was piped to six houses.

Five bed roomed, Bank House Farm, Stoke St Milborough dates back to 1750. The farmhouse is mainly Georgian style with a Victorian addition. It stands at the foot of the Brown Clee Hill surrounded by a gently sloping 146 acres of pasture and woodland. The Carter family farmed here for over fifty years in the C20.

Moor Hall.

Originally named the Moor and built for William Walcot in 1793. Moor Hall was owned by Hon F. G. Hamilton-Russell who was Lord of the Manor and his tenant was George Stepney Gulston in 1909. It is now Grade II listed.

Langley farm, on the boundary of Stanton Lacy consists of a C16 farmhouse with 340 acres of farmland on the Plymouth Estate. The beautiful black and white house is now a listed building. It has been farmed by the Brereton family since 1908 and has recently achieved high level status in game conservation. Mrs Grace Brereton, (mother to John and Peter) seen here with Mr and Mrs Mellor in 1949. Mr Mellor was agent for the Plymouth Estates.

Stanton Lacy old Post Office was originally the village pub named the Craven Arms. It was named after the Earl of Craven who owned much of the area. It was last recorded as a pub in 1861 and later was to become a shop before becoming a post office and is now a private house. The thatch was replaced with a shingled roof in the 1950s.

St Peters Church, Stanton Lacy.

Foundations of the first original Saxon church at Stanton Lacy suggest a date of 680 A.D. Originally the village was named 'Staunton', later Stanton, to become 'Stanton Lacy', named after the Lacy family, lords of the manor. Stanton Lacy's church of St Peter dates to about 1050, with later rebuilding in the 13th and 16th centuries. You can still see original Saxon stonework in the west and north walls of the church. There are Saxon pilaster strips in the north wall of the nave, also in the east and west walls of the north transept. The Victorians could not resist 'improving' the church, and to them we owe the current vividly coloured stained glass windows, the altar, and the carved reredos of Caen stone. The church is built to a cruciform plan, with a sturdy central tower. The nave and north transept are the oldest parts of the church, both retaining many late Saxon or early Norman features, while the tower is Early English and the south aisle C14. There is a blocked north doorway which probably dates to the late Saxon period. Above the interior face of the doorway is a carved panel, dated the C11-C12, while another fragment of worn C12 carving has been reset in the wall over the north doorway. The nave arcade is C14, as is the octagonal font and canopied piscina.

Born in Stanton Lacy, **William Charles Williams VC** (15 September 1880 – 25 April 1915) was a British recipient of the Victoria Cross, the highest and most prestigious award for gallantry in the face of the enemy that can be awarded to British and Commonwealth forces. He was born in Stanton Lacy , but raised in Chepstow, Wales. He joined the Boys Service in Portsmouth in 1895 and was promoted to the boys' first class in 1896, Seaman in 1898 and Able Seaman in 1901. He joined the Royal Navy as a young sailor, but left in 1910, joining the Royal Naval Reserve and working in the police force and in a steel works in Newport. He rejoined the Navy in 1914 on being mobilised at the start of the First World War. During his career, he served on eighteen different ships, some more than once. He was 34 years old when the following deed took place for which he was awarded the VC. On 25th April, 1915 during the landing on V Beach, Cape Helles, Gallipoli, Turkey. Williams, with three other men were assisting Edward Unwin, the commander of their ship, HMS River Clyde (previously the SS River Clyde) at the work of securing the lighters. Williams held on to a rope for over an hour, standing chest deep in the sea, under continuous enemy fire. He was eventually dangerously wounded and later killed by a shell whilst his rescue was being effected by the commander who described him as the bravest sailor he had ever met. There are two memorials to him in Chepstow - a painting by Charles Dixon of the events in the Dardanelles, hanging in St Mary's Church and a naval gun from the German submarine SM UB-91 presented by King George V, which stands in the town's main square beside the War Memorial.

William Charles Williams' medals.

Stanton Lacy Vicarage.

A large, mellow coloured stone building that stands proud, with its large chimney and fancy stone window surrounds. 56 acres of glebe land are attached, all in the gift of the trustees of the Clive family. Rev Robert Foulkes lived at the vicarage 1660-1678. He and his wife took in a young lady lodger who he took advantage of and a baby was born. He murdered the baby and on 31st January 1679 he was hung for his crime.

Stanton Lacy Primitive Methodist Chapel.

Stanton Lacy had two Primitive Methodist Chapels and two Wesleyan Chapels in the parish. The village once had a school, shop, blacksmith, post office, pub, mill, cobbler and wheelwright but they are no more.

Manor Farm, Stanton Lacy.
This lovely picture of the manor farm workers erecting a hay rick with the help of a horse drawn Shropshire cart was a typical country scene in the early 1900s.

The Atora Suet Advertising Campaign ran from 1923 until 1932 and here we see Reg Lippet driving his two Hereford bullocks that travelled throughout the area advertising Atora Suet.

Training Bullocks.

William Deakin, the Gravel farm at Downton bred the two Hereford bullocks named Sinbad and Sailor. Reg Lippet was their trainer, teaching them how to pull the cart correctly. Reg had spent the early part of his life training horses to pull gun carriages in WWI.

Shoeing the Bullocks.

The bullocks once went as far as Scotland and of course on the stone roads they would need shoes. George Jones the blacksmith at Bromfield would be called on to catch and shoe the bullocks. As they are cloven footed they would need 8 shoes for each bullock. Care would have to be taken as the bullocks were likely to kick out when being caught.

Bromfield Blacksmith Shop.

Here we see blacksmiths George Randall on left and George Jones leading out Sinbad and Sailor after being shod.

Twelve Apostles, Bromfield.

Bromfield once had a landmark of great interest – 12 poplar trees transported by stagecoach from London and planted to commemorate the birth of Louisa Florential Hodges in 1822. She was the 13th child of the Rev. Thomas Hodges and lived to be 93 years old. These poplars were known locally as the Twelve Apostles and curiously one of the trees fell on a Good Friday. The remaining trees were damaged by gales and twelve replacement poplars were planted by Bromfield blacksmith William Teague and his eldest son in the early 1900's. Eleven by the old road bridge and one in the estate yard, but this one never flourished. They came down in 1968 when the A49 was realigned. In 1964 Bromfield's vicar was Rev Leland Blashford Snell, father of famous explorer, John Blashford Snell.

Henry Hill Hickman (1800-1830) was born the third son of a tenant farmer on the Earl of Plymouth's estate at Lady Halton.

Lady Halton Farm.

At 16, Henry Hickman studied medicine in Edinburgh and opened a practice in Corve Street, Ludlow at the age of 21, in 1821. He travelled to France in 1828, trying to persuade King Charles to back him in his findings but soon returned to England disillusioned that no one would believe in his work. He opened a practice at 18 Teme Street, Tenbury Wells and later at Shifnal. Hickman worked hard to prove his theory that you could suspend animation by giving gas and that the patient would feel no pain when operated on. Sadly he died of TB in 1830 aged thirty and it was not until 1930 that his brilliant work was recognised. He was then known as one of the fathers of anaesthesia. He is buried in Bromfield churchyard.

Bromfield Races.

This postcard shows Bromfield Races in the early days. In the C14, soldiers stationed at Ludlow Castle used to use Bromfield to match their horse against others. The Ludlow National Hunt racecourse opened on August 27th 1729 and is one of the oldest in the UK. It was first used for flat racing and jumps were added later. Henry Herbert, of nearby Oakley Park was the main sponsor of the races and of the evening entertainment. In 1871 the Race Club was formed, with members paying an annual subscription of £5 plus an entrance fee of £5. The club had a limit of 400 members and in 1907 there were 360 members. This stand was built in 1907; the Jubilee Stand was built in 2002 and stood alongside. The racecourse is about 1.5 miles long and 16 race meetings are held each year. 2,000 American soldiers were camped at the racecourse during WWII. 1,900 years after 4,500 Roman soldiers were camped there under canvas. The twenty acre racecourse site also houses the Bromfield Golf Club which was founded in 1889. The 70 par, 18 hole course is 6,277 yards long and was remodelled by James Braid in 1922.

Two well known ladies at Bromfield Races in 1980.

Bromfield's church of St Mary on the left, on the right is the old Priory gate.

The church contains a painted ceiling by Thomas Francis in the chancel, depicting angels and clouds plus religious texts painted on streamers. The work of art was completed in 1672. The C14 Priory Gate on the right was the entrance to the Benedictine Priory. It has been used as a courtroom, village school and a reception room. The priory itself was built in 1155 but dissolved by Henry VIII in 1538. It was purchased by Charles Foxe in 1564 and he converted the Priory into a house but in the C17 the house was destroyed.

The gipsy wedding of Ivor and Selina Lock at Bromfield Church in 1937.

Rev Summerhayes performed the wedding ceremony of second cousins, Selina and Ivor Locke, in 1937. They were gypsies living in their caravans near to Bromfield bridge. Selina had been knocked down by a car a week before and Mrs Summerhayes had made her a veil that covered the seven stitches in her forehead. Her father gave her away and her sister was the bridesmaid. The couple were forced to move to Craven Arms when the ground at Bromfield became flooded.

The mid C19 Bromfield corn mill and bakehouse on the Plymouth estate alongside the river Teme at Bromfield is currently being restored, with the weir as part of a hydro-electricity generation scheme.

Bromfield Post Office.

The name of Bromfield derives from the broom shrubs that grew in the area surrounding the village. This is the village Post Office where William Wadely was sub postmaster and village tailor. Mrs Wadely offered afternoon teas in the garden in the early 1900s. The confluence of the river Onny and the river Teme is close by.

This was a familiar sight, **The Corvedale bus alongside Ludlow Town Hall in the 1940s and 50s.** The Victorian era and the coming of the combustion engine were soon to lead to the introduction of the motor car, quickly followed by the omnibus. Very soon, in the late 1920s and 1930s small country bus operators were beginning to establish themselves by providing an essential service between many rural communities. Ludlow and its feeder villages were not to be left behind. Here, the roots of the independent bus operators lay across the border in North Herefordshire. In the 1930's much of the local bus network was operated by two individuals; firstly, by Mr E.E. Williams of Wormelow, secondly, by Mr E. Morgan, the owner of Wye Valley Motor Services. From a business viewpoint there was to be some coming together of these two individuals later in the decade, resulting in a mutually agreed exchange of service routes. The agreement lead to Mr Williams taking over the operations within Shropshire from a new base at Kingsley Garage, Ludlow. The new enterprise was titled the Corvedale Motor Company and it came into being in March 1939. The inevitable difficulties associated with the WWII conflict were stoically met and the bus fleet expanded. Yet further increased growth took place with the acquisition of various small operators including Sydney Cadwallader of Corfton, Holts of Orleton, Bert Green of Hopton Cangeford, Sidney Smith of Bitterley and Francis Jones of Cleobury North. All this enlargement had taken place before 1950 and had resulted in an expansion of Corvedale services to Much Wenlock, Ditton Priors and Tenbury Wells on a daily basis plus a longer distance service to Worcester. Considerable indirect help was forthcoming in maintaining passenger revenue and this came about by the closure of the railways' country branch lines and local stations. The Craven Arms to Much Wenlock service was the first to close in 1951, followed by the Wofferton to Bewdley and the Cleobury Mortimer to Ditton Priors branch lines in 1965. Additionally it is important to remember that all intermediate stations on the Shrewsbury to Hereford route were closed at this time with the exception of Church Stretton and Ludlow. It was a fact that if you hadn't got a car, and many didn't at this time, you were obliged to utilise the local bus services to get from place to place and people did in considerable numbers. E.E. Williams continued to expand with the purchase of new and second hand vehicles throughout the 1950s and early 1960s but finally decided to 'call it a day' in 1965 when he sold the business to the Yeoman's family enterprise at Canon Pyon.

Corvedale Motor Company Ticket.

Corve Bridge 1896.

On May 13th 1896 Corve Bridge in Ludlow was swept away in a great flood. Just six days later, this picture was taken of the workmen re-opening the road with a temporary bridge. It was eventually replaced with stone.

Corve Bridge.

An early Corve bridge with five arches was mentioned in 1540. The present bridge (pictured), with three arches, was built in 1787 by the corporation. It is built in fine ashlar stone, the centre arch being twenty feet wide and the arches either side are each seventeen feet wide. The foundation is said to have been made with stones from the old chapel of St Leonard.

A Caddick postcard showing **Ludlow from the Whitcliffe.** Ludlow was so named after the Welsh meaning of Hlud- Hlaw, 'Hill by a loud river'. The Whitcliffe name is derived from the white limestone cliffs. The cliff was formed by the receding Ice Age, creating the gorge between the Whitcliffe and Ludlow town. The castle stands proudly over the town and has done since Walter de Lacy commenced the building of it in 1086. The early C14 saw the castle change ownership to Roger Mortimer, first Earl of the Marches, the most powerful man in England at that time. He enlarged the castle and made it into his Palace. In 1772 the Earls of Powys rented the castle and in 1811 purchased it. It has remained in their ownership and is now owned by the trustees of the Powys Castle Estate on behalf of the family of the Earls. It is now Grade II listed and a scheduled monument.

Castle Square in Ludlow taken from the castle gate. The 26 pounder cannon is a trophy from the Crimean war at the siege of Sevastopol in 1855. Many cannons were captured and presented to towns throughout Britain. The 136 feet high church tower in the background is that of St Laurence's Church, Shropshire's largest parish church and often called the Cathedral of the Marches. Originally it was an early C11 church that was rebuilt in 1199, with major restoration in 1433-1471. The church interior was restored in 1861. The Johan Snetzler organ, costing £1,000, was donated by Henry Herbert, first Earl of Powys in 1764. A.E. Housman 1859-1936 has his ashes buried in the church grounds. The building in the centre of the picture is the town hall that had replaced a previous one built in 1702. The town hall in the picture was built to commemorate the jubilee of Queen Victoria in 1887 at a cost of £6,000. Sadly it was demolished in 1986 and, as yet, not been replaced. The building on the extreme right is the castle lodge which was originally built early in the C13 and used as a prison in the early C16. It was rebuilt in stone, combining three properties, in 1580, by Thomas Sackford who was Keeper of the Prisons in the Marches of Wales. The timber upper storey was added later.

Castle Lodge interior, Ludlow.

One of the largest areas of C13 oak panelling in England adorns the Lodge interior. Catherine of Aragon resided here whilst she was married to Prince Arthur and she later married his brother, Henry VIII. In later years it was a hotel until WWII. In 1999 it was opened to the public and in 2011 it was for sale at £590,000.

This superb sculpture by Captain Adrian Jones stood above the entrance, inside the Twon Hall.

Princess Mary in Ludlow.

The Mayor of Ludlow, Mr George Woodhouse bidding farewell to Princess Mary at Corve Bridge, after her visit to Ludlow in 1908.

Gaius Smith's grocery shop at Kings Street in Ludlow.

Gaius Smith was the largest grocery chain in the district, with nine shops in South Shropshire plus several delivery vans that delivered to isolated villages. Gaius was one of five brothers from Tenbury Wells and all had learned the butchery trade. Gaius Smith opened a shop in Ludlow in 1875 and grew the business to this prestigious 'stores' by 1884. He was well respected in the community and was elected mayor of Ludlow 1898-9. This postcard shows his shop in 1920. The company prospered well into the mid C20 before closing.

The Angel Hotel in Broad Street was mentioned in 1551 when it was the principal hostelry in Ludlow with its 18 bed rooms and stabling for 18 horses. They had their own coach named the *Aurora* which made the trip to London in 27 hours in 1820. Lord Nelson stayed at the hotel in 1802 with his lady friend and her husband, Emma and Sir William Hamilton. Nelson addressed a crowd from the bay window whilst staying there.

Lucian Bonaparte.

Lucian Bonaparte, younger brother of Napoleon Bonaparte, dined at the Angel hotel in 1811. He was captured at sea whilst seeking refuge in America. He was held on parole at Dinham House in Ludlow, along with his wife, seven children and twenty three servants.

The Bull Ring in Ludlow named after the area where cattle and sheep were sold in the C17. W H Smith's originally started business in London in1792. It was started by Henry Walton Smith but it was his son, William Henry Smith, which took over in 1812 and renamed the business. In 1846 William renamed it again to W H Smith and Son, as his son became a partner. It was to become the first chain store in the world. They came to Ludlow in the 1880s, situated at the railway station. They opened this branch in the Bull Ring in 1905 and the outlet remained there until it closed, well into the C20. In 2012 a brand new W H Smith opened in King Street. The Wainwright shop on the corner was established in 1879, selling leather goods and, later, jewellery. On the extreme left is the Bull Ring Tavern, which, in the past, had been a butcher's, milliners and taxidermist, before becoming Dawes & Bowen's wine and spirit merchants in 1880. In 1901 it was The Vaults and had an off licence. It was renamed Ye Olde Bull Ring Tavern in the 1930's. At the time of this photo the chemist, George Woodhouse, was occupying the black and white building next door, taken over by Boots the chemist in 1965. It was originally The Bear Inn which opened in 1635. The plain building next door behind the dog was first known as New Wine Cellars in the C18, later The Wine Vaults and then Keysell's. You may think that Ludlow is all pubs, well, at their peak there were some fifty five ale houses in the town but you can be assured that there is plenty more to Ludlow, (such as a variety of shops, the 500 historic buildings, museum and cafes), making it well worth market town to visit – as thousands do annually.

Ludlow Post Office workers in 1948.

The mayor of Ludlow, Mr William James Brown, is seated next to postmaster Mr R.E. Cole. This was the presentation day of the Safety First medals to the postmen who had travelled 90,000 miles without an accident.

A massive crowd receiving a Royal visit at the Buttercross in Ludlow in 1922.

The Buttercross was built at a cost of £1,000 in 1744 by William Baker of Audlem, a well respected architect and building contractor who also built Montgomery Town Hall in 1748. It replaced the 'The Cross', a 1570 timber framed building that marked the centre of Ludlow and was where a cupola housed the bell from St Leonards Church. King Street, Broad Street and High Street meet here. The Buttercross first floor has had several uses; a boy's charity school, the Council Chambers and a history museum from 1953 until 1993. The ground floor was used as a market place where traders sold their produce and it is still in use today. The building is now grade I listed and £100,000 was spent on restoration recently. The building to the right of the lamppost is Bodenham's, a ladies and gents outfitters corner shop, one of the oldest in Britain. William Bodenham opened the shop in 1860 but when it came time for his sons to take over they fell out and two thirds of the shop was sold off. At present, the fifth generation of the Bodenham family run the shop, Roger Curry and his wife Monica. He is the great great grandson of William Bodenham.

Feathers Hotel.

One of five hundred listed buildings in Ludlow, the Feathers Hotel dates back to 1619. Built by Rees Jones, a successful local attorney, its world famous timber facade was adorned with motifs of ostrich feathers, which gave the hotel its name. The town's sympathies lay with the monarchy and these feathers depicted the traditional badge of the Prince of Wales who had been enthroned in 1616 and who would later become King Charles I. During the English Civil War in the 1640s, Ludlow remained loyal to the King and it is thought that Royalist soldiers would have lodged at 'the Feathers'. Thomas Jones, son of Rees Jones, fought in the King's army and after the war he returned to Ludlow to convert The Feathers into an inn. It remained an inn for the next 200 years, giving food, ale and rest to locals and strangers alike, as well as serving as a cock-fighting venue. It also played an important part in local politics, as prospective candidates gave impassioned speeches from its balcony before inviting the electorate inside for a persuasive drink! The Feathers Inn became The Feathers Hotel in 1863 and along with Ludlow Castle has become the focal point for tourists visiting the historic town.

On the opposite side of Corve Street from the Feathers stands the **Bull Hotel.** A building stood there in 1343 and most probably in 1199 when St Laurence's church was built. The first mention of the Bull Inn was in 1580, certainly the oldest Inn in Ludlow. It withstood a fire in 1693 started by protesters of a Presbyterian meeting being held there. In 1794 a fire destroyed the front of the timber fronted inn and it was replaced by a rendered facade, as it is today.

De Greys in Broad Street, Ludlow.

was reputed to be one of the finest tea rooms in Britain. Parts of the building are C14 and in the late C16 it was an inn named 'The Swann'. In 1900, Herbert Smith had his boot and shoe makers business there. That was taken over by Freeman Hardy & Willis and in the 1920s De Greys opened their cafe-restaurant. Sadly, as this book is being written, De Greys closed its doors for the last time on Saturday 18th January, 2014, with the author having, as he puts it: his "last supper there". It reopened under new management in 2014.

George Foster's lorry from Leominster being used as a platform for the open air religious rally on Whitcliffe, Ludlow, in 1922. In the week George would sell and deliver corn, wool, seeds and cattle food. On a Sunday he was the preacher at the Gospel Hall or an open air rally. Next to the organ is George preaching with a large congregation listening.

The gipsy family of Smith's camped on Whitcliffe. Gypsies would park their horse drawn caravans near to Ludlow so that they could walk into town to sell their pegs and trinkets.

Castle Garage, Ludlow.
Castle Garage was founded in the 1930's by J D Parsonage. This picture of the staff in the 1950s is when it was owned by Jack Price, who later moved the garage to Corve Street.

Caddick alongside the river Corve with his converted mobile shop.
He took several photos of Ludlow including this wonderful shot of the castle.

Burway Bridge, Coronation Avenue, Ludlow.

At 2am on 26th June, 2007 the Burway Bridge in Ludlow, that had stood there since 1927, collapsed and fell into the raging River Corve. The river had rose 1.6m in three hours and scoured away the bridge's foundations causing it to collapse. The A49 road had a sixteen metre gap and was no longer passable. The council bin men filled 4,000 sandbags to help nearby houses combat the flooded river. A flock of sheep that had huddled on high ground could not be reached and perished in the floods.

Burway Bridge, Ludlow.

As you can see, the bridge was irrepairable and the severed gas main was left hanging in the air in 2007. A 31.5m bailey bridge was erected in six weeks. Eighteen months later, a brand new Burway Bridge was completed by contractors McPhillips at a cost of £1m. Sol and Doreen Pearce, who had lost their home to the floods, cut the ribbon at the bridge opening ceremony in March 2009.

On 27th June 2007, one day after the Burway Bridge collapsed.

Two walls of 57A Corve Street succumbed to the continual pounding of the flooded river and fell into the water leaving the rest of the house unsafe. Sol and Doreen Pearce had lived at the house for forty one years but decided to move to a new home at nearby Whitbatch Close. The remainder of the Corve Street house was demolished. Thirty other Corve Street residents were temporally moved from their homes in case of further flooding. Tesco cafe was commandeered and later the Ludlow Leisure Centre to house the victims of the floods. One cannot imagine that such a disaster could be caused from a river that was merely a puddle just seventeen miles away.

The river Corve is just 200 yards from the confluence with the river Teme at this point. It is a picturesque scene, alongside the Linney footbridge and weir, with St Laurence's Church in the background.

The river Corve confluence.

Here, just north of Ludlow Castle, we see the confluence of the rivers Corve and Teme. The Corve has finally reached its seventeen mile journey's end from Bourton. The interesting hamlets and villages that border the river are still there, why not pick up this book and visit some of them. You won't be disappointed.

The river Teme then continues down around Ludlow Castle at Linney, in view of the Church and Castle.

The Teme continues down to the weir at Dinham, under Dinham bridge, before travelling down to the south of Worcester where it joins the longest river in the British Isles, the 220 mile long River Severn. The Severn's source is on the side of Plynlimon in Wales and its mouth forms an estuary at the Bristol Channel before reaching the sea. The author hopes you have enjoyed 'the dawdle' with him along the river Corve, as much as he has.

The true Alchemists do not change lead into gold, they change the world into words.